To:

_____

$\mathcal{B}$lessed is the nation whose
God is the LORD.

Psalm 33:12

From:

_____

If my people,

who are called by my name,

will humble themselves

and pray and seek my face

and turn from their wicked ways,

then will I hear from heaven

and will forgive their sin

and will heal their land.

2 Chronicles 7:14

God Bless America: Prayers and Reflections for Our Country
Copyright 1999 by Zondervan
ISBN 0-310-80063-3

Requests for information should be addressed to:
        Inspirio, The gift group of Zondervan
        Grand Rapids, Michigan 49530
        http://www.inspiriogifts.com

Senior Editor: Gwen Ellis
Creative Director: Patricia Matthews
Project Editor: Pat Matuszak
Compilation: Susan Johnson
Graphic Designer: Jody DeNeef
Cover Photography:
   Tony Stone Images—Tom Tracy
Interior Photography:
   Tony Stone Images—Oldrich Karasek, Doug Armand, Joseph
   Nettis, Robert Shafer, Jon Ortner, Cosmo Condina, Darrell
   Gulin, Vito Palmisano, Tom Tracy, The Image Bank—Steve
   Dunwell

Printed in the United States of America

01 02 03 04 05 / WP / 8 7 6 5

GOD BLESS AMERICA

Prayers & Reflections
For Our Country

inspirio

The gift group of Zondervan

𝒥NDEX OF SCRIPTURE

CONTENTS

PRAYER

Those who hope in the LORD

will renew their strength.

They will soar on wings like eagles;

they will run and not grow weary,

they will walk and not be faint.

Isaiah 40:31

PRAYER

A Prayer for Our Country

Almighty God, you have given us this great land as our heritage. We humbly pray that we may always remember your generosity and faithfully do your will. Bless our land with honest industry, truthful education and an honorable way of life. Defend our liberties and strengthen the resolve of the people who have come from throughout the world to make America their home. Lead us to choose the harder right instead of the easier wrong. Help us to appreciate the opportunities that are ours as we struggle to bring harmony to an unsettled world. May we balance our concern for justice with a willingness to display mercy, and may our concern for security be tempered with a willingness to take risks which will produce worthwhile change for the good of all people. O Lord, we pray for your guidance as we work together for the best interest of our communities, our nation, our world, and the ultimate goal of peace. When times are prosperous, let our hearts be thankful and in troubled times may our deepest trust be in you. Amen.

Chaplains' Service Book of Prayers

Thankful to Be an American

Alone among the great nations of the world, Americans define their identity outside the boundaries of geography or common ethnic ancestry. For us there is no fatherland; nor can most of us trace our ancestors back five and six generations or more, as the British, French, Norwegians, and Irish so proudly do.

We are instead a people who have come from every corner of the globe, most of us in the last century, and all of us in pursuit of a most noble and remarkable vision—that in this land men and women could live in freedom and liberty with their God-given rights respected.

It is, therefore, a common creed, not common ancestral roots, which binds us together. That creed was best expressed in the Declaration of Independence which announced, "We hold these truths to be self-evident, that all men are created equal, that they are endowed by their Creator with certain unalienable Rights, that among these are Life, Liberty and the pursuit of Happiness." Americans are forever indebted to those who pledged their lives and fortunes and sacred honor to make this experiment in ordered liberty possible.

"Gratitude," G. K. Chesterton wrote, "is the mother of all virtues." As Americans we have reason to be filled with gratitude at all times; gratitude to God who gave us the opportunity to come to this land and to live in freedom, gratitude to our Founding Fathers who set forth those principles that constitute our creed, and gratitude to following generations who have defended us.

This should inspire and encourage in Americans a sense of civic duty and responsibility far greater than loyalty to state or ancestry. When in the Korean War my turn came to serve my country, I saw it as not only my duty, but a privilege. Grateful for my liberty, I could do no less than my duty to protect it.

The history of the past 225 years shows what a difference loyalty to principled beliefs can make. America has never sought wars of expansion. It has sought to liberate and restore

those it has defeated. It has shared its bounty
and wealth with the poor. It has rescued the
suffering. It has done this not because the
fatherland orders it, but because our devotion
to human dignity and human liberty demands it.
America is different—it is a vision, a noble idea—
and for that extraordinary difference, Americans
should give thanks to God each day and pledge
anew to do their duty out of gratitude to Him
and to our Founding Fathers.

—Charles W. Colson, Chairman
Prison Fellowship Ministries

A Foundation of
PRAYER

A Foundation of Prayer

The first Day of Prayer was declared by the Continental Congress in 1775.

I therefore beg leave to move—
    That henceforth prayers, imploring the assistance of Heaven and its blessing on our deliberations, be held in this assembly every morning before we proceed to business; and that one or more of the clergy of this city be requested to officiate in that service. —*Ben Franklin*

In 1952 both Houses of Congress called upon the President to set aside a day each year as National Day of Prayer.

Prayer has indeed been a vital force in the growth and development of this Nation. It would certainly be appropriate if ... the People of this country were to unite in a day of prayer each year ... reaffirming in a dramatic manner the deep religious conviction which has prevailed throughout the history of the United States.
                                                —*Judiciary Committee's Report*

In 1988, President Ronald Reagan signed a bill marking the first Thursday of May a National Day of Prayer.

On our National Day of Prayer, then, we join together as people of many faiths to petition God to show us His mercy and His love, to heal our weariness and uphold our hope, that we might live ever mindful of His justice and thankful for His blessing.
                                                      —*Ronald Reagan*

Presidential

PRAYERS

Prayers of United States Presidents

Almighty God: We make our earnest prayer that
Thou wilt keep the United States in Thy holy
protection: that Thou wilt incline the hearts of the
citizens to cultivate a spirit of subordination and
obedience to government, and entertain a brotherly
affection and love for one another and for their
fellow citizens of the United States at large.

And finally that Thou wilt most graciously be
pleased to dispose us all to do justice, to love
mercy, and to demean ourselves with that charity,
humility, and pacific temper of mind which were
the characteristics of the Divine Author of our
blessed religion, and without a humble imitation of
whose example in these things we can never hope
to be a happy nation.

Grant our supplication, we beseech Thee,
through Jesus Christ our Lord. Amen.

—George Washington

I pray God I may be given the wisdom and the
prudence to do my duty in the true spirit of this
great people. *—Woodrow Wilson*

In entering upon this great office I must humbly invoke the God of our fathers for wisdom and firmness to execute its high and responsible duties in such a manner as to restore harmony and ancient friendship among the people of the several States and to preserve our free institutions throughout many generations.   *—James Buchanan*

So we pray to Him now for the vision to see our way clearly—to see the way that leads to a better life for ourselves and for all our fellow men—to the achievement of His will to peace on earth.

—Franklin D. Roosevelt

Almighty God, as we stand here, at this moment, my future associates in the executive branch of the government join me in beseeching that Thou will make full and complete our dedication to the service of the people in this throng and their fellow citizens everywhere.

Give us, we pray, the power to discern clearly right from wrong and allow all our works and actions to be governed thereby and by the laws of this land.

Especially we pray that our concern shall be for all the people, regardless of station, race, or calling. May cooperation be permitted and be the mutual aim of those who, under the concept of our

Constitution, hold to differing political beliefs, so that all may work for the good of our beloved country and for Thy glory. Amen.

—Dwight Eisenhower

I would like to have my frequent prayer answered that God let my life be meaningful in the enhancement of His kingdom and that my life might be meaningful in the enhancement of the lives of my fellow human beings. *—Jimmy Carter*

Today, we utter no prayer more fervently than the ancient prayer for peace on Earth.

—Ronald Reagan

Heavenly Father, we bow our heads and thank You for Your love. Accept our thanks for the peace that yields this day and the shared faith that makes its continuance likely. Make us strong to do Your work, willing to heed and hear Your will, and write on our hearts these words: "Use power to help people." For we are given power not to advance our own purposes, nor to make a great show in the world, nor a name. There is but one just use of power, and it is to serve people. Help us to remember it, Lord. Amen.   *—George Bush*

Scriptures about Prayer

I urge, then, first of all, that requests, prayers, intercession and thanksgiving be made for everyone—for kings and all those in authority, that we may live peaceful and quiet lives in all god-liness and holiness. This is good, and pleases God our Savior, who wants all men to be saved and to come to a knowledge of the truth.

—*1 Timothy 2:1–4*

Jesus said, "For where two or three come together in my name, there am I with them."

—*Matthew 18:20*

Let us not be like others, who are asleep, but let us be alert and self-controlled. For those who sleep, sleep at night, and those who get drunk, get drunk at night. But since we belong to the day, let us be self-controlled, putting on faith and love as a breastplate, and the hope of salvation as a helmet. For God did not appoint us to suffer wrath but to receive salvation through our Lord Jesus Christ. He died for us so that, whether we are awake or asleep, we may live together with him. Therefore encourage one another and build each other up, just as in fact you are doing. Now we ask you, brothers, to respect those who work hard among you, who are over you

in the Lord and who admonish you. Hold them in
the highest regard in love because of their work.
Live in peace with each other. And we urge you,
brothers, warn those who are idle, encourage the
timid, help the weak, be patient with everyone.
Make sure that nobody pays back wrong for wrong,
but always try to be kind to each other and to
everyone else. Be joyful always; pray continually;
give thanks in all circumstances, for this is God's will
for you in Christ Jesus.

—1 Thessalonians 5:6–18

What other nation is so great as to have their gods
near them the way the LORD our God is near us
whenever we pray to him?   *—Deuteronomy 4:7*

We do not know what we ought to pray for, but the
Spirit himself intercedes for us with groans that
words cannot express.   *—Romans 8:26*

And pray in the Spirit on all occasions with all
kinds of prayers and requests. With this in mind,
be alert and always keep on praying for all the
saints.   *—Ephesians 6:18*

Pray for us. We are sure that we have a clear conscience and desire to live honorably in every way.
—Hebrews 13:18

Do not be anxious about anything, but in everything, by prayer and petition, with thanksgiving, present your requests to God. And the peace of God, which transcends all understanding, will guard your hearts and your minds in Christ Jesus.
—Philippians 4:6–7

Devote yourselves to prayer, being watchful and thankful . . . that God may open a door for our message, so that we may proclaim the mystery of Christ.
—Colossians 4:2–3

O LORD, I call to you; come quickly to me.
    Hear my voice when I call to you.
May my prayer be set before you like incense;
    may the lifting up of my hands be like the
    evening sacrifice.

—Psalm 141:1–2

Teach me your way, O LORD,
    and I will walk in your truth;
give me an undivided heart,
    that I may fear your name.

—Psalm 86:11

You hold me by my right hand.
You guide me with your counsel, . . .
Whom have I in heaven but you?
   And earth has nothing I desire besides you.
                                    —Psalm 73:23–25

Come, let us bow down in worship,
   let us kneel before the LORD our Maker;
for he is our God
   and we are the people of his pasture,
   the flock under his care.
                                    —Psalm 95:6–7

Praise the LORD, all you nations;
   extol him, all you peoples.
For great is his love toward us,
   and the faithfulness of the LORD endures
   forever.
Praise the LORD.
                                    —Psalm 117:1–2

Let us then approach the throne of grace with
confidence, so that we may receive mercy and find
grace to help us in our time of need.
                                    —Hebrews 4:16

Jesus told his followers, "This, then, is how you should pray:

" 'Our Father in heaven,
hallowed be your name,
your kingdom come,
your will be done
   on earth as it is in heaven.
Give us today our daily bread.
Forgive us our debts,
   as we also have forgiven our debtors.
And lead us not into temptation,
but deliver us from the evil one.'"

—*Matthew 6:9–13*

Then Jesus told his disciples a parable to show them that they should always pray and not give up.

—*Luke 18:1*

Jesus replied, "… I tell you the truth, if you have faith as small as a mustard seed, you can say to this mountain, 'Move from here to there' and it will move. Nothing will be impossible for you."

—*Matthew 17:20*

Be joyful in hope, patient in affliction, faithful in prayer.

—*Romans 12:12*

PRAYER

Praise the LORD.
I will extol the LORD with all my heart
in the council of the upright and in the
assembly.
Great are the works of the LORD;
they are pondered by all who delight in them.
Glorious and majestic are his deeds,
and his righteousness endures forever.
He has caused his wonders to be remembered;
the LORD is gracious and compassionate.
He provides food for those who fear him;
he remembers his covenant forever.

—Psalm 111:1–5

Praise the LORD.
Praise, O servants of the LORD,
praise the name of the LORD.
Let the name of the LORD be praised,
both now and forevermore.
From the rising of the sun to the place where it sets,
the name of the LORD is to be praised.
The LORD is exalted over all the nations,
his glory above the heavens.
Who is like the LORD our God,
the One who sits enthroned on high,
who stoops down to look
on the heavens and the earth?

—Psalm 113:1–6

To you, O LORD, I lift up my soul;
   in you I trust, O my God.

—Psalm 25:1–2

Sovereign Lord, you made the heaven and the
earth and the sea, and everything in them.

—Acts 4:24

Not to us, O LORD, not to us
   but to your name be the glory,
   because of your love and faithfulness.

—Psalm 115:1

If any of you lacks wisdom, he should ask God,
who gives generously to all without finding fault,
and it will be given to him.   *—James 1:5*

Scriptures about Thankfulness

Give thanks to the LORD, call on his name;
make known among the nations what he has
done.

—1 Chronicles 16:8

Let the heavens rejoice, let the earth be glad;
let them say among the nations,
"The LORD reigns!"

—1 Chronicles 16:31

Give thanks to the LORD, for he is good;
his love endures forever.

—1 Chronicles 16:34

Let them give thanks to the LORD for his
unfailing love
and his wonderful deeds for men.
Let them exalt him in the assembly of the people
and praise him in the council of the elders.

—Psalm 107:31–32

Just as you received Christ Jesus as Lord, continue
to live in him, rooted and built up in him,
strengthened in the faith as you were taught, and
overflowing with thankfulness.   *—Colossians 2:6–7*

Praise the LORD, all you nations;
   extol him, all you peoples.
For great is his love toward us,
   and the faithfulness of the LORD endures
      forever.
Praise the LORD.

                                        —*Psalm 117:1*

Shout for joy to the LORD, all the earth.
   Worship the LORD with gladness;
   come before him with joyful songs.
Know that the LORD is God.
   It is he who made us, and we are his;
   we are his people, the sheep of his pasture.
Enter his gates with thanksgiving
   and his courts with praise;
   give thanks to him and praise his name.
For the LORD is good and his love endures forever;
   his faithfulness continues through all
      generations.

                                        —*Psalm 100:1–5*

We ought always to thank God for you, brothers,
and rightly so, because your faith is growing more
and more, and the love every one of you has for
each other is increasing.   —*2 Thessalonians 1:3*

Scriptures about

THANKFULNESS

Be joyful always; . . . give thanks in all
circumstances, for this is God's will for you in
Christ Jesus.   *—1 Thessalonians 5:16, 18*

I thank my God every time I remember you. In all
my prayers for all of you, I always pray with joy
because of your partnership in the gospel from the
first day until now, being confident of this, that he
who began a good work in you will carry it on to
completion until the day of Christ Jesus.

—Philippians 1:3–6

You are my God, and I will give you thanks;
    you are my God, and I will exalt you.
Give thanks to the LORD, for he is good;
    his love endures forever.

—Psalm 118:28–29

Now to the King eternal, immortal, invisible, the
only God, be honor and glory for ever and ever.
Amen.   *—1 Timothy 1:17*

You are worthy, our Lord and God,
   to receive glory and honor and power,
for you created all things,
   and by your will they were created
   and have their being.

—Revelation 4:11

Worthy is the Lamb, who was slain,
to receive power and wealth and wisdom and
   strength
and honor and glory and praise!

—Revelation 5:12

Scriptures about Faith

Without faith it is impossible to please God,
because anyone who comes to him must believe
that he exists and that he rewards those who
earnestly seek him.   *—Hebrews 11:6*

Jesus answered, "I am the way and the truth and
the life. No one comes to the Father except
through me."   *—John 14:6*

Those who know your name will trust in you,
   for you, LORD, have never forsaken those who
   seek you.

—Psalm 9:10

Be still, and know that I am God;
   I will be exalted among the nations,
   I will be exalted in the earth.

—Psalm 46:10

The eyes of the LORD are on the righteous
   and his ears are attentive to their cry.

—Psalm 34:15

Be still before the LORD and wait patiently for him.
—Psalm 37:7

May God be gracious to us and bless us
and make his face shine upon us,
that your ways may be known on earth,
your salvation among all nations.
—Psalm 67:1–2

If you do not stand firm in your faith,
you will not stand at all.
—Isaiah 7:9

Open the gates
that the righteous nation may enter,
the nation that keeps faith.
You will keep in perfect peace
him whose mind is steadfast,
because he trusts in you.
Trust in the LORD forever,
for the LORD, the LORD, is the Rock eternal.
—Isaiah 26:2–4

Jesus replied, "I tell you the truth, if you have faith and do not doubt, not only can you do what was done to the fig tree, but also you can say to this mountain, 'Go, throw yourself into the sea,' and it will be done." —*Matthew 21:21*

Consider how the lilies grow. They do not labor or spin. Yet I tell you, not even Solomon in all his splendor was dressed like one of these. If that is how God clothes the grass of the field, which is here today, and tomorrow is thrown into the fire, how much more will he clothe you, O you of little faith! And do not set your heart on what you will eat or drink; do not worry about it. For the pagan world runs after all such things, and your Father knows that you need them. But seek his kingdom, and these things will be given to you as well. —*Luke 12:27–31*

Will not God bring about justice for his chosen ones, who cry out to him day and night? Will he keep putting them off? I tell you, he will see that they get justice, and quickly. However, when the Son of Man comes, will he find faith on the earth? —*Luke 18:8*

You and I may be mutually encouraged by each other's faith. —*Romans 1:12*

This righteousness from God comes through faith in Jesus Christ to all who believe. There is no difference, for all have sinned and fall short of the glory of God, and are justified freely by his grace through the redemption that came by Christ Jesus.

—Romans 3:22–24

Since we have been justified through faith, we have peace with God through our Lord Jesus Christ, through whom we have gained access by faith into this grace in which we now stand. And we rejoice in the hope of the glory of God.

—Romans 5:1–2

Faith comes from hearing the message, and the message is heard through the word of Christ.

—Romans 10:17

Remember your leaders, who spoke the word of God to you. Consider the outcome of their way of life and imitate their faith.   *—Hebrews 13:7*

Now faith is being sure of what we hope for and certain of what we do not see. This is what the ancients were commended for. By faith we understand that the universe was formed at God's command, so that what is seen was not made out of what was visible.   *—Hebrews 11:1–3*

Reflections about Prayer

O Lord, Almighty and everlasting God, by Thy
Word Thou hast created the heaven, and the earth,
and the sea; blessed and glorified be Thy Name,
and praised be Thy Majesty, which hath deigned to
use us, Thy humble servants, that Thy holy Name
may be proclaimed in this second part of the earth.

—Christopher Columbus

To pray effectively we must want what God wants—
that and only that is to pray in the will of God. And
no petition made in the will of God was ever
refused.

—A. W. Tozer

Lord, teach us to pray. Some of us are not skilled
in the art of prayer. As we draw near to thee in
thought, our spirits long for thy Spirit, and reach
out for thee, longing to feel thee near.

—Peter Marshall

I have been driven many times upon my knees by
the overwhelming conviction that I had nowhere
else to go. My own wisdom, and that of all about
me, seemed insufficient for that day.

—Abraham Lincoln

Reflections about
PRAYER

Prayer is the one hand with which we grasp the Invisible; fasting the other, with which we let loose and cast away the visible.   —*Andrew Murray*

We must wait on Him moment by moment for the fulfillment of His promised blessings and must trust Him to obtain them for us. So that in a fuller sense than ever before we are nothing and Christ is all. The only prayer that accomplishes anything is that which was offered in "the power and reality of the life of Christ in the soul." The Spirit must make intercession in us, if we expect to have power with God.   —*Hannah Whitall Smith*

Only when we have knelt before God, can we stand before men.   —*Anonymous*

He that is down, needs fear no fall;
He that is low, no pride;
He that is humble ever shall
Have God to be his guide.

—*John Bunyan*

Reflections about
PRAYER

Humility is perfect quietness of heart. It is to have no trouble. It is never to be fretted or irritated or sore or disappointed. It is to expect nothing, to wonder at nothing that is done to me. It is to be at rest when nobody praises me and when I am blamed or despised. It is to have a blessed home in the Lord, where I can go in and shut the door and kneel to my Father in secret, and am at peace as in the deep sea of calmness when all around and above is trouble. —*Andrew Murray*

Jesus himself has shown us by his own example that prayer and fasting are the first and most effective weapons against the forces of evil.
—*Pope John Paul II*

When we work, we work. When we pray, God works. —*J. Hudson Taylor*

Every work of God can be traced to some kneeling form. —*D. L. Moody*

The faith we bring to prayer must include a trust that God is able to hear our prayers and that He is disposed to answer them. Yet when God says no to our requests, this faith also trusts in His wisdom.
—*R. C. Sproul*

Prayer can obtain everything: it can open the windows of heaven, and shut the gates of hell; it can put a holy constraint upon God, and detain an angel until he leave a blessing.

—Mrs. Charles Cowman

Be thou my vision, O Lord of my heart
Naught be all else to me, save that thou are:
Thou my best thought, by day or by night,
Waking or sleeping, thy presence my light.

—Ancient Irish Prayer, Translation, Mary Byrne

Our God, we acknowledge that you are the Lord of the nations; that kingdoms, kings and queens, and political leaders rise and fall within the purpose and plan that you have for this universe. We thank you for the freedoms that we enjoy as part of this experiment in democracy that we call the United States. We thank you for the freedom of religion; that we can gather to sing of your faithfulness, to give of our resources, to open your Word, to listen to your voice; and we do it without harassment, intimidation, threat of imprisonment, or persecution.

—Edward Dobson

Reflections about
PRAYER

God wants us to ask Him for the impossible! God can do things that man cannot do. He would not be God if this were not so. That is why He has graciously made prayer a law of life. "If you will ask . . . I will do." This inviting promise from the Lord means that He will do for us what we cannot do for ourselves; He will do for others what we cannot do for them—if we but ask Him.

—*Mrs. Charles Cowman*

Entering thus solemnly into covenant with each other, we may reverently invoke and confidently expect the favor and help of Almighty God—that He will give to me wisdom, strength, and fidelity, and to our people a spirit of fraternity and a love of righteousness and peace.   —*Benjamin Harrison*

My prayer is that God will grant each one of us today a new beginning. With all my heart, I pray that every single one of us will determine, right now, in this hour, that we will stand firm, that we will join the mighty army of the Lord, outfitted with spiritual armor, fully prepared to engage in the battle for the soul of America. And to overcome the world for Christ.   —*James Kennedy*

We know, our Father, that at this desperate hour in world affairs, we need thee. We need thy strength, thy guidance, thy wisdom. There are problems far greater than any wisdom of man can solve. What shall our leaders do in such an hour?

May thy wisdom and thy power come upon those whom have been entrusted leadership. May the responsibility lie heavily on their hearts, until they are ready to acknowledge their helplessness and turn to thee. Give to them the honesty, the courage, and the moral integrity to confess that they don't know what to do. Only then can they lead us as a nation beyond human wisdom to thee, who alone hast the answer.

Lead us to this high adventure. Remind us that a "mighty fortress is our God"— not a hiding place where we can escape for an easy life, but rather an arsenal of courage and strength the mightiest of all, who will march beside us into the battle for righteousness and world brotherhood.

—*Peter Marshall*

I Need Thee Ev'ry Hour

> I need Thee ev'ry hour,
> Most gracious Lord;
> No tender voice like Thine
> Can peace afford.
> I need Thee, oh! I need Thee;
> Ev'ry hour I need Thee;
> O bless me now, my Savior
> I come to Thee.
>
> I need Thee ev'ry hour,
> Stay Thou near by;
> Temptations lose their pow'r
> When Thou art nigh.
> I need Thee, oh! I need Thee;
> Ev'ry hour I need Thee;
> O bless me now, my Savior
> I come to Thee.

—*Mrs. Annie Hawks*

Sweet Hour of Prayer

Sweet hour of pray'r, sweet hour of pray'r!
That calls me from a world of care,
And bids me at my Father's throne
Make all my wants and wishes known:
In seasons of distress and grief,
My soul has often found relief;
And oft escaped the tempter's snare,
By Thy return, sweet hour of pray'r!

—William W. Walford

Be thankful for the least gift, so shalt thou be meant to receive greater. *—Thomas à Kempis*

My fellow-citizens, no people on earth have more cause to be thankful than ours, and this is said reverently, in no spirit of boastfulness in our own strength, but with gratitude to the Giver of Good who has blessed us with the conditions which have enabled us to achieve so large a measure of well-being and of happiness. *—Theodore Roosevelt*

Reflections about

PRAYER

**On October 3, 1863, an Act of Congress designated an
annual National Day of Thanksgiving as proclaimed by
President Abraham Lincoln**

I do, therefore, invite my fellow citizens in every
part of the United States ... to set apart and
observe the last Thursday of November next as a
day of Thanksgiving and Praise to our beneficent
Father who dwelleth in the heavens.... [it is]
announced in the Holy Scriptures and proven by
all history, that those nations are blessed whose
God is the Lord.... It has seemed to me fit and
proper that God should be solemnly, reverently
and gratefully acknowledged, as with one heart and
one voice, by the whole American people.

—Abraham Lincoln

It must be felt that there is no national security but
in the nation's humble acknowledged dependence
upon God and His overruling providence.

—President John Adams

O God, our Father, we pray that the people of America, who have made such progress in material things, may now seek to grow in spiritual understanding.

For we have improved means, but not improved ends. We have better ways of getting there, but we have no better places to go. We can save more time, but are not making any better use of the time we save.

We need Thy help to do something about the world's true problems—the problem of lying, which is called propaganda; the problem of selfishness, which is called self-interest; the problem of greed, which is often called profit; the problem of license disguising itself as liberty; the problem of lust, masquerading as love; the problem of materialism, the hook which is baited with security.

Hear our prayers, O Lord, for the spiritual understanding which is better than political wisdom, that we may see our problems for what they are. This we ask in Jesus' name. Amen.

—*Peter Marshall*

Love of prayer is one of the marks of the Spirit.

—*Andrew Murray*

The Holy Spirit is God at work.

—*D.L. Moody*

We wish to pray in the Spirit and at the same time after the flesh, and this is impossible.

—*Andrew Murray*

The wings of prayer carry high and far.

—*Anonymous*

Prayer is ACTS
  Adoration
  Confession
  Thanksgiving
  Supplication

Prayer includes praise and thanksgiving, intercession and petition, meditation, and confession. In prayer we focus fully on our God.

—*Charles Swindoll*

  I ought to pray—
I ought to always pray—
I should not grow faint in praying—

—*Mrs. Charles Cowman*

A feeling of real need is always a good enough
reason to pray.   *—Hannah Whitall Smith*

In the beginning of the contest with Great Britain,
when we were sensible of danger, we had daily
prayers in this room for divine protection. Our
prayers were heard, and they were graciously
answered ... Have we now forgotten this powerful
friend? Or do we no longer need his assistance?

I have lived a long time, and the longer I live,
the more convincing proofs I see of this truth:
"that God governs the affairs of man." And if a
sparrow cannot fall to the ground without his
notice, is it probable that an empire can rise
without his aid?

—Ben Franklin to the
Constitutional Congress 1787

FREEDOM

The Liberty Bell

Proclaim liberty through all

the land and to all the

inhabitants thereof.

This inscription engraved
on the Liberty Bell in 1753
is taken from Leviticus 25:10.

FREEDOM

The Declaration of Independence

We hold these truths to be self-evident,
that all men are created equal;
that they are endowed by their Creator
with certain inalienable rights;
that among these are life, liberty,
and the pursuit of happiness.

For the support of this declaration,
with a firm reliance on the protection
of the Divine Providence,
we mutually pledge to each other, our lives,
our fortunes, and our sacred honor.

July 4, 1776

Scriptures about Freedom in Christ

Then it was said among the nations,
"The LORD has done great things for them."
The LORD has done great things for us,
and we are filled with joy.

—Psalm 126:2–3

In Christ and through faith in him we may
approach God with freedom and confidence.

—Ephesians 3:12

Jesus said, "Come to me, all you who are weary
and burdened, and I will give you rest. Take my
yoke upon you and learn from me, for I am gentle
and humble in heart, and you will find rest for
your souls. For my yoke is easy and my burden is
light." *—Matthew 11:28–30*

I will walk about in freedom,
for I have sought out your precepts.
I will speak of your statutes before kings
and will not be put to shame,
for I delight in your commands
because I love them.
I lift up my hands to your commands, which I love,
and I meditate on your decrees.

—Psalm 119:45–48

Scriptures about
FREEDOM

Now the Lord is the Spirit, and where the Spirit of
the Lord is, there is freedom.

—2 Corinthians 3:17

Jesus said, "If you hold to my teaching, you are
really my disciples. Then you will know the truth,
and the truth will set you free."   *—John 8:31–32*

It is for freedom that Christ has set us free.

—Galatians 5:1

The Spirit of the Sovereign LORD is on me,
    because the LORD has anointed me
    to preach good news to the poor.
He has sent me to bind up the brokenhearted,
    to proclaim freedom for the captives
    and release from darkness for the prisoners.

—Isaiah 61:1

The creation waits in eager expectation for the
sons of God to be revealed. . . . in hope that the
creation itself will be liberated from its bondage to
decay and brought into the glorious freedom of the
children of God.   *—Romans 8:19–21*

He who was a slave when he was called by the
Lord is the Lord's freedman; similarly, he who was
a free man when he was called is Christ's slave.
You were bought at a price; do not become slaves
of men.   *—1 Corinthians 7:22–23*

Now the Lord is the Spirit, and where the Spirit of
the Lord is, there is freedom. And we, who with
unveiled faces all reflect the Lord's glory, are being
transformed into his likeness with ever-increasing
glory, which comes from the Lord, who is the
Spirit.   *—2 Corinthians 3:17–18*

You, my brothers, were called to be free. But do
not use your freedom to indulge the sinful nature;
rather, serve one another in love. The entire law is
summed up in a single command: "Love your
neighbor as yourself."   *—Galatians 5:13–14*

If the Son sets you free, you will be free indeed.
                                          —John 8:36

Scriptures about God's Protection

I lift up my eyes to the hills—
  where does my help come from?
My help comes from the LORD,
  the Maker of heaven and earth.
He will not let your foot slip—
  he who watches over you will not slumber.
The LORD watches over you—
  the LORD is your shade at your right hand;
the sun will not harm you by day,
  nor the moon by night.
The LORD will keep you from all harm—
  he will watch over your life;
the LORD will watch over your coming and going
  both now and forevermore.
                              —Psalm 121:1–3, 5–8

The eyes of the LORD range throughout the earth
to strengthen those whose hearts are fully
committed to him.   *—2 Chronicles 16:9*

God is our refuge and strength,
  an ever-present help in trouble.

                              —Psalm 46:1

The LORD surrounds his people
both now and forevermore.

                              —Psalm 125:2

God has said,
> "Never will I leave you;
> never will I forsake you."

So we say with confidence,
> "The Lord is my helper; I will not be afraid.
> What can man do to me?"

—Hebrews 13:5–6

He guards the course of the just
> and protects the way of his faithful ones.

—Proverbs 2:8

He is my loving God and my fortress,
> my stronghold and my deliverer,
> my shield, in whom I take refuge.

—Psalm 144:2

What, then, shall we say in response to this? If God is for us, who can be against us?

—Romans 8:31

The LORD your God is with you,
> he is mighty to save.

He will take great delight in you,
> he will quiet you with his love,
> he will rejoice over you with singing.

—Zephaniah 3:17

"As for God, his way is perfect;
    the word of the LORD is flawless.
He is a shield
    for all who take refuge in him.
For who is God besides the LORD?
    And who is the Rock except our God?
It is God who arms me with strength
    and makes my way perfect."

—2 Samuel 22:31–33

See, the LORD your God has given you the land. Go up and take possession of it as the LORD, the God of your fathers, told you. Do not be afraid; do not be discouraged. *—Deuteronomy 1:21*

I will say of the LORD, "He is my refuge and
        my fortress,
    my God, in whom I trust."

—Psalm 91:2

So do not fear, for I am with you;
    do not be dismayed, for I am your God.
    I will strengthen you and help you;
    I will uphold you with my righteous right hand.

—Isaiah 41:10

Many nations will come and say,

> "Come, let us go up to the mountain of the LORD,
>   to the house of the God of Jacob.
> He will teach us his ways,
>   so that we may walk in his paths."
> The law will go out from Zion,
>   the word of the LORD from Jerusalem.

> He will judge between many peoples
>   and will settle disputes for strong nations
>   far and wide.

> They will beat their swords into plowshares
>   and their spears into pruning hooks.
> Nation will not take up sword against nation,
>   nor will they train for war anymore.

> Every man will sit under his own vine
>   and under his own fig tree,
> and no one will make them afraid,
>   for the LORD Almighty has spoken.

> All the nations may walk
>   in the name of their gods;
> we will walk in the name of the LORD
> our God for ever and ever.

—*Micah 4:2–5*

Scriptures about God's Guidance

But when he, the Spirit of truth, comes, he will guide you into all truth. He will not speak on his own; he will speak only what he hears, and he will tell you what is yet to come.   *—John 16:13*

If the LORD delights in a man's way,
   he makes his steps firm;
though he stumble, he will not fall,
   for the LORD upholds him with his hand.
               —Psalm 37:23–24

May the Lord direct your hearts into God's love and Christ's perseverance.   *—2 Thessalonians 3:5*

Guide me in your truth and teach me,
   for you are God my Savior,
   and my hope is in you all day long.
               —Psalm 25:5

Send forth your light and your truth,
   let them guide me.
               —Psalm 43:3

You guide me with your counsel,
   and afterward you will take me into glory.
               —Psalm 73:24

Since you are my rock and my fortress,
  for the sake of your name lead and guide me.
                                    —Psalm 31:3

I guide you in the way of wisdom
  and lead you along straight paths.
                                    —Proverbs 4:11

For this God is our God for ever and ever;
  he will be our guide even to the end.
                                    —Psalm 48:14

May the nations be glad and sing for joy,
  for you rule the peoples justly
  and guide the nations of the earth.
                                    —Psalm 67:4

Teach us to number our days aright,
  that we may gain a heart of wisdom.
                                    —Psalm 90:12

Trust in the LORD with all your heart
  and lean not on your own understanding;
in all your ways acknowledge him,
  and he will make your paths straight.
Do not be wise in your own eyes;
  fear the LORD and shun evil.

                                    —Proverbs 3:5–7

See, I have taught you decrees and laws as the
LORD my God commanded me, so that you may
follow them in the land you are entering to take
possession of it. Observe them carefully, for this
will show your wisdom and understanding to the
nations, who will hear about all these decrees and
say, "Surely this great nation is a wise and
understanding people."   *—Deuteronomy 4:5–6*

The fear of the LORD is the beginning of wisdom,
    and knowledge of the Holy One is understanding.
                                      —Proverbs 9:10

You are in Christ Jesus, who has become for us
wisdom from God—that is, our righteousness,
holiness and redemption.   *—1 Corinthians 1:30*

Everyone who hears these words of mine and puts
them into practice is like a wise man who built his
house on the rock. The rain came down, the
streams rose, and the winds blew and beat against
that house; yet it did not fall, because it had its
foundation on the rock.

                                      —Matthew 7:24–25

My salvation and my honor depend on God;
    he is my mighty rock, my refuge.

—Psalm 62:7

The Holy Spirit also testifies to us about this. First
    he says:
"This is the covenant I will make with them
    after that time, says the Lord.
I will put my laws in their hearts,
    and I will write them on their minds."
Then he adds:
"Their sins and lawless acts
    I will remember no more."
And where these have been forgiven, there is no
    longer any sacrifice for sin.

—Hebrews 10:15–18

He will call upon me, and I will answer him;
    I will be with him in trouble,
    I will deliver him and honor him.

—Psalm 91:15

The statutes of the LORD are trustworthy,
    making wise the simple.

—Psalm 19:7

The mouth of the righteous man utters wisdom,
    and his tongue speaks what is just.
The law of his God is in his heart;
    his feet do not slip.

—Psalm 37:30–31

I walk in the way of righteousness,
    along the paths of justice.

—Proverbs 8:20

Every prudent man acts out of knowledge.

—Proverbs 13:16

The LORD gives wisdom to the wise
    and knowledge to the discerning.

—Daniel 2:21

If you call out for insight
    and cry aloud for understanding,
and if you look for it as for silver
    and search for it as for hidden treasure,
then you will understand the fear of the LORD
    and find the knowledge of God.
For the LORD gives wisdom,
    and from his mouth come knowledge and
        understanding.

—Proverbs 2:3–6

To the man who pleases him, God gives wisdom,
knowledge and happiness.

—Ecclesiastes 2:26

The LORD will guide you always;
  he will satisfy your needs in a sun-scorched land
  and will strengthen your frame.
You will be like a well-watered garden,
  like a spring whose waters never fail.

—Isaiah 58:11

Blessed is the man
  who makes the LORD his trust.

—Psalm 40:4

Reflections about Freedom

The God who gave us life gave us liberty at the
same time.
                              —Thomas Jefferson

The cause of freedom is the cause of God.
                              —William Lisle Bowles

Man is really free only in God, the source of his
freedom.
                              —Sherwood Eddy

Religion, virtue, whate'er we call
A blessing—freedom is the pledge of all.
                              —William Cowper

Liberty is the mother of virtue.
                              —Mary Wollstonecraft

Freedom is one of the deepest and noblest
aspirations of the human spirit.   *—Ronald Reagan*

We know what works: Freedom works. We know
what's right: Freedom is right.   *—George Bush*

Freedom of religion, freedom of the press, and
freedom of person under the protection of the
habeas corpus, these are the principles that guided
our steps through an age of revolution and
reformation.   *—Thomas Jefferson*

Freedom of religion is written into the constitution. No state in the world has been so strongly influenced by biblical Christianity.

—Operation World

But I say to all men, what we have achieved in liberty, we will surpass in greater liberty. Steadfast in our faith in the Almighty, we will advance toward a world where man's freedom is secure.

—Harry S. Truman

I still believe there can be a day when we will have true freedom: a day when we can all get along regardless of our race. This is not a dream. It is alive within the ability of us all.   *—Rosa Parks*

Freedom and the dignity of the individual have been more available and assured here than in any other place on Earth.   *—Ronald Reagan*

Under the eternal urge of freedom we became an independent Nation.   *—Calvin Coolidge*

Is life so dear, or peace so sweet, as to be purchased at the price of chains and slavery? Forbid it, Almighty God! I know not what course others may take but as for me; give me liberty or give me death.   *—Patrick Henry*

America Confesses

Our Father, bring to the remembrance of Thy people Thine ancient and time-honored promise: "If my people, which are called by my name, shall humble themselves, and pray, and seek my face, and turn from their wicked ways; then will I hear from Heaven, and will forgive their sin, and will heal their land."

We—This company of Thy people assembled— would begin now to meet the conditions that will enable Thee to fulfill Thy promise.

May all of America come to understand that right-living alone exalteth a nation, that only in Thy will can peace and joy be found. But, Lord, this land cannot be righteous unless her people are righteous, and we, here gathered, are part of America. We know that the world cannot be changed until the hearts of men are changed. Our hearts need to be changed.

We therefore confess to Thee that:

Wrong ideas and sinful living have cut us off from Thee.

We have been greedy.

We have sought to hide behind barricades of selfishness; shackles have imprisoned the great heart of America.

We have tried to isolate ourselves from the
  bleeding wounds of a blundering world.
In our self-sufficiency we have sought not
  Thy help.
We have held conferences and ignored
  Thee completely.

—Peter Marshall

Our values, our principles, and our determination
to succeed as a free and democratic people will
give us a torch to light the way. And we will survive
and become the stronger—not only because of a
patriotism that stands for love of country, but a
patriotism that stands for love of people.

—Gerald Ford

The Bible is the cornerstone of liberty.

—Thomas Jefferson

God grants liberty only to those who love it, and
are always ready to guard and defend it.

—Daniel Webster

The power in the dream God dreams for you is
stronger than the weight of tradition, mightier than
the force of history. The right kind of dream can
liberate an entire nation or emancipate a life from
any negative circumstances.   *—Wintley Phipps*

Reflections about
Freedom

Posterity—you will never know how much it has cost my generation to preserve your freedom. I hope you will make good use of it.

—John Quincy Adams

We Americans of today, together with our allies, are passing through a period of supreme test. It is a test of our courage—of our resolve—of our wisdom—our essential democracy.

—Franklin D. Roosevelt

We cannot overestimate the fervent love of liberty, the intelligent courage, and the sum of common sense with which our fathers made the great experiment of self-government.

—James A. Garfield

You gain strength, courage, and confidence by every experience in which you really stop to look fear in the face . . . you must do the thing you think you cannot do.　　　*—Eleanor Roosevelt*

Events have brought our American democracy to new influence and new responsibilities. They will test our courage, our devotion to duty, and our concept of liberty.　　　*—Harry S. Truman*

Hold fast to the Bible as the sheet anchor of your liberties; write its precepts on your heart and practice them in your lives. To the influence of this Book we are indebted for the progress made, and to this we must look as our guide in the future.

—Ulysses S. Grant

In Christ we are not promised "freedom from," instead we are promised that through divinely designed restrictions we are free to find what we yearn for: fulfillment and meaning in life. Slaves to Christ, we become truly free.   *—Larry Richards*

My fellow Americans: ask not what your country can do for you—ask what you can do for your country. My fellow citizens of the world: ask not what America will do for you, but what together we can do for the freedom of man.

—John F. Kennedy

Reflections about

FREEDOM

Under this Constitution the boundaries of freedom
have been enlarged, the foundations of order and
peace have been strengthened, and the growth of
our people in all the better elements of national
life has indicated the wisdom of the founders and
given new hope to their descendants.

—*James Garfield*

My Country, 'Tis of Thee

My country, 'tis of Thee,
Sweet land of liberty
Of thee I sing;
Land where my fathers died,
Land of the pilgrim's pride,
From every mountain side
Let freedom ring.

Our fathers' God to Thee,
Author of liberty,
To Thee we sing;
Long may our land be bright
With freedom's holy light;
Protect us by Thy might,
Great God our King.

—*Samuel Francis Smith*

Battle Hymn of the Republic

Glory! glory, hallelujah!
Glory! glory, hallelujah!
Glory! glory, hallelujah!
His truth is marching on.

I have seen him in the watch-fires of a hundred
    circling camps,
They have builded him an altar in the evening
    dews and damps;
I can read his righteous sentence by the dim
    and flaring lamps—
His day is marching on.

He has sounded forth the trumpet that shall
    never call retreat;
He is sifting out the hearts of men before his
    judgment-seat;
Oh, be swift, my soul, to answer him! be
    jubilant, my feet!
Our God is marching on.

In the beauty of the lilies Christ was born across
    the sea,
With a glory in his bosom that transfigures
    you and me;
As he died to make men holy, let us die to make
    men free,
While God is marching on.

                     —*Julia Ward Howe*

LEADERSHIP

Be men worthy of respect, sincere, not

indulging in much wine, and not

pursuing dishonest gain....

Keep hold of the deep truths of the

faith with a clear conscience.

Those who have served well gain an

excellent standing and great assurance

in their faith in Christ Jesus.

1 Timothy 3:8–9, 13

LEADERSHIP

Executive Oath of Office

"I do solemnly swear (or affirm) that I will faithfully execute the Office of President of the United States, and will to the best of my ability, preserve, protect and defend the Constitution of the United States."

United States Constitution,
Article II, Section 1, Clause 8

Remember your leaders, who spoke the word of God to you. Consider the outcome of their way of life and imitate their faith. Jesus Christ is the same yesterday and today and forever.

Hebrews 13:7–8

74

Scriptures about Responsibility

I have taken an oath and confirmed it,
    that I will follow your righteous laws.

—Psalm 119:106

From everyone who has been given much, much
will be demanded; and from the one who has been
entrusted with much, much more will be asked.

—Luke 12:48

Love the L ORD your God with all your heart and
with all your soul and with all your strength. These
commandments that I give you today are to be
upon your hearts. Impress them on your children.
Talk about them when you sit at home and when
you walk along the road, when you lie down and
when you get up. Tie them as symbols on your
hands and bind them on your foreheads. Write
them on the doorframes of your houses and on
your gates.   *—Deuteronomy 6:5–9*

Commit to the L ORD whatever you do,
    and your plans will succeed.

—Proverbs 16:3

Scriptures about
RESPONSIBILITY

Everyone must submit himself to the governing authorities, for there is no authority except that which God has established. The authorities that exist have been established by God.

—Romans 13:1

Be careful that you do not forget the LORD your God, failing to observe his commands, his laws and his decrees. *—Deuteronomy 8:11*

All the ways of the LORD are loving and faithful
  for those who keep the demands of his covenant.

—Psalm 25:10

But if anyone obeys his word, God's love is truly made complete in him. This is how we know we are in him: Whoever claims to live in him must walk as Jesus did. *—1 John 2:5–6*

A wise man has great power, and a man of knowledge increases strength. *—Proverbs 24:5*

Who is wise and understanding among you? Let him show it by his good life, by deeds done in the humility that comes from wisdom. *—James 3:13*

The wise in heart accept commands.

—Proverbs 10:8

Scriptures about Obedience

Your statutes are wonderful;
   therefore I obey them.

—Psalm 119:129

"Your hearts must be fully committed to the LORD
our God, to live by his decrees and obey his
commands, as at this time."   *—1 Kings 8:61*

My son, do not forget my teaching,
   but keep my commands in your heart,
for they will prolong your life many years
   and bring you prosperity.

—Proverbs 3:1–2

Observe the commands of the LORD your God,
walking in his ways and revering him.

—Deuteronomy 8:6

"If you follow my decrees and are careful to obey
my commands, I will send you rain in its season,
and the ground will yield its crops and the trees of
the field their fruit. Your threshing will continue
until grape harvest and the grape harvest will
continue until planting, and you will eat all the
food you want and live in safety in your land."

—Leviticus 26:3–5

Jesus said, "If you love me, you will obey what I command."
—*John 14:15*

And this is his command: to believe in the name of his Son, Jesus Christ, and to love one another as he commanded us. Those who obey his commands live in him, and he in them. And this is how we know that he lives in us: We know it by the Spirit he gave us.
—*1 John 3:23–24*

This is how we know that we love the children of God: by loving God and carrying out his commands.
—*1 John 5:2*

Seek the LORD, all you humble of the land,
 you who do what he commands.
Seek righteousness, seek humility.
—*Zephaniah 2:3*

Whoever serves me must follow me; and where I am, my servant also will be. My Father will honor the one who serves me.
—*John 12:26*

Be joyful always; give thanks in all circumstances, for this is God's will for you in Christ Jesus.
—*1 Thessalonians 5:16, 18*

Scriptures about Respect

Now the overseer must be above reproach, the husband of but one wife, temperate, self-controlled, respectable, hospitable, able to teach. He must also have a good reputation with outsiders. *—1 Timothy 3:2, 7*

In everything set them an example by doing what is good. *—Titus 2:7*

Remind the people to be subject to rulers and authorities, to be obedient, to be ready to do whatever is good, to slander no one, to be peaceable and considerate, and to show true humility toward all men. *—Titus 3:1–2*

So Pharaoh asked them, "Can we find anyone like this man, one in whom is the spirit of God?" Then Pharaoh said to Joseph, "Since God has made all this known to you, there is no one so discerning and wise as you. You shall be in charge of my palace, and all my people are to submit to your orders." *—Genesis 41:38–40*

Do not be overcome by evil, but overcome evil
with good. Everyone must submit himself to the
governing authorities, for there is no authority
except that which God has established. The
authorities that exist have been established by God.

Consequently, he who rebels against the
authority is rebelling against what God has
instituted, and those who do so will bring judgment
on themselves. For rulers hold no terror for those
who do right, but for those who do wrong. Do you
want to be free from fear of the one in authority?
Then do what is right and he will commend you.
For he is God's servant to do you good. But if you
do wrong, be afraid, for he does not bear the sword
for nothing. He is God's servant, an agent of wrath
to bring punishment on the wrongdoer. Therefore,
it is necessary to submit to the authorities, not only
because of possible punishment but also because of
conscience.

This is also why you pay taxes, for the
authorities are God's servants, who give their full
time to governing. Give everyone what you owe
him: If you owe taxes, pay taxes; if revenue, then
revenue; if respect, then respect; if honor, then
honor.   *—Romans 12:21–13:7*

"In your unfailing love you will lead
the people you have redeemed.
In your strength you will guide them
to your holy dwelling."

—Exodus 15:13

The king's heart is in the hand of the LORD;
he directs it like a watercourse wherever he
pleases.

—Proverbs 21:1

The wise inherit honor.   *—Proverbs 3:35*

Show proper respect to everyone: Love the
brotherhood of believers, fear God, honor the king.

—1 Peter 2:17

He has declared that he will set you in praise, fame
and honor high above all the nations he has made
and that you will be a people holy to the LORD
your God, as he promised.   *—Deuteronomy 26:19*

O LORD, our God, other lords besides you have
rules over us,
but your name alone do we honor.

—Isaiah 26:13

Scriptures about Wisdom

Trust in the LORD with all your heart
    and lean not on your own understanding;
in all your ways acknowledge him,
    and he will make your paths straight.

—Proverbs 3:5–6

The fear of the LORD is the beginning of wisdom;
    all who follow his precepts have good
        understanding. To him belongs eternal praise.

—Psalm 111:10

Blessed is the man who finds wisdom,
    the man who gains understanding.

—Proverbs 3:13

A man's wisdom gives him patience;
    it is to his glory to overlook an offense.

—Proverbs 19:11

Do not forsake wisdom, and she will protect you;
    love her, and she will watch over you.
Wisdom is supreme; therefore get wisdom.
Though it cost all you have, get understanding.

—Proverbs 4:6–7

Brothers, choose seven men from among you who are known to be full of the Spirit and wisdom. We will turn this responsibility over to them.

—Acts 6:3

Give me wisdom and knowledge, that I may lead this people, for who is able to govern this great people of yours? *—2 Chronicles 1:10*

If any of you lacks wisdom, he should ask God, who gives generously to all without finding fault, and it will be given to him. But when he asks, he must believe and not doubt, because he who doubts is like a wave of the sea, blown and tossed by the wind. *—James 1:5–6*

A wise man has great power,
and a man of knowledge increases strength.

—Proverbs 24:5

Teach us to number our days aright,
that we may gain a heart of wisdom.

—Psalm 90:12

Who is wise and understanding among you? Let
him show it by his good life, by deeds done in the
humility that comes from wisdom.   *–James 3:13*

The mouth of the righteous brings forth wisdom.
–Proverbs 10:31

How much better to get wisdom than gold, to
choose understanding rather than silver!
–Proverbs 16:16

The wise in heart accept commands.
–Proverbs 10:8

It is because of him that you are in Christ Jesus,
who has become for us wisdom from God–that is,
our righteousness, holiness and redemption.
–1 Corinthians 1:30

Therefore everyone who hears these words of mine
and puts them into practice is like a wise man who
built his house on the rock. The rain came down,
the streams rose, and the winds blew and beat
against that house; yet it did not fall, because it
had its foundation on the rock. *–Matthew 7:24–25*

Reflections about Godly Leadership

It is impossible rightly to govern the world without God and the Bible.   *—George Washington*

Our job in government, and your job as leaders in the law, is to strengthen the faith of the people—in the resolute protection of their rights, and in the effective delivery of justice.

    —Dan Quayle at the bicentennial of the Bill of Rights

In the beginning the Old World scoffed at our experiment; today our foundations of political and social belief stand unshaken, a precious inheritance to ourselves, an inspiring example of freedom and civilization to all mankind.

    —Warren G. Harding

Under this covenant of justice, liberty, and union we have become a nation—prosperous, great, and mighty.   *—Lyndon Baines Johnson*

The foundation of our national policy will be laid in the pure and immutable principles of private morality, and the preeminence of free government will be exemplified by all the attributes which can win the affections of its citizens and command the respect of the world.   *—George Washington*

Reflections about
LEADERSHIP

The Bible is the rock on which our republic rests.
>   —*Andrew Jackson*

The more profoundly we study this wonderful
Book and the more closely we observe its divine
precepts, the better citizens we will become and
the higher will be the destiny of our nation.
>   —*William McKinley*

The church was and is the foundation of our
community. It became our strength, our refuge,
and our haven.   —*Rosa Parks*

To us as a people it has been granted to lay the
foundations of our national life in a new continent.
>   —*Theodore Roosevelt*

The foundations of our society and our government rest so much on the teachings of the Bible
that it would be difficult to support them if faith in
these teachings would cease to be practically
universal in our country.   —*Calvin Coolidge*

God's Word, contained in the Bible, has furnished
all necessary rules to direct our conduct.
>   —*Noah Webster*

Under this Constitution the boundaries of freedom
have been enlarged, the foundations of order and
peace have been strengthened, and the growth of
our people in all the better elements of national
life has indicated the wisdom of the founders and
given new hope to their descendants.

—James Garfield

A union depending not upon the constraint of
force, but upon the loving devotion of a free
people; "and that all things may be so ordered and
settled upon the best and surest foundations that
peace and happiness, truth and justice, religion
and piety, may be established among us for all
generations." *—Rutherford B. Hayes*

I accept my part with single-mindedness of
purpose and humility of spirit, and implore the
favor and guidance of God in His Heaven.

—Warren G. Harding

In the swift rush of great events, we find ourselves
groping to know the full sense and meaning of
these times in which we live. In our quest of
understanding, we beseech God's guidance.

—Dwight D. Eisenhower

With a firm reliance upon the wisdom of Omnipotence to sustain and direct me in the path of duty which I am appointed to pursue, I stand in the presence of this assembled multitude of my countrymen to take upon myself the solemn obligation to the best of my ability to preserve, protect, and defend the Constitution of the United States.
                                                            —*James Knox Polk*

God gives us biblical principles not so that we can arrange our lives according to our taste, but so that we can know how God wants us to live.
                                                            —*Larry Crabb*

Let us go forth to lead the land we love, asking His blessing and His help, but knowing that here on earth God's work must truly be our own.
                                                            —*John F. Kennedy*

I assume the arduous and responsible duties of President of the United States, relying upon the support of my countrymen and invoking the guidance of Almighty God.   —*William McKinley*

Obedience to God is the most infallible evidence of sincere and supreme love to him.
                                                            —*Nathanael Emmons*

This occasion is not alone in the administration of the most sacred oath which can be assumed by an American citizen. It is a dedication and consecration under God to the highest office in service of our people. I assume this trust in the humility of knowledge that only through the guidance of Almighty Providence can I hope to discharge its ever-increasing burdens. *—Herbert Hoover*

While this duty rests upon me I shall do my utmost to speak their purpose and to do their will, seeking Divine guidance to help us each and every one to give light to them that sit in darkness and to guide our feet into the way of peace.

—Franklin D. Roosevelt

Henceforth I learn that to obey is best,
And love with fear the only God.

—John Milton

To obey God in some things and not in others shows an unsound heart. Childlike obedience moves toward every command of God, as the needle points where the loadstone draws.

—Thomas Watson

In a republic the first rule for the guidance of the citizen is obedience to law. *—Calvin Coolidge*

Reflections about
LEADERSHIP

An investment in knowledge always pays the best interest. —*Benjamin Franklin*

Nothing sets a person so much out of the devil's reach as humility. —*Jonathan Edwards*

The higher a man is in grace, the lower he will be in his own esteem. —*Charles Haddon Spurgeon*

He Leadeth Me! O Blessed Thought!

He leadeth me! O blessed thought!
O words with heav'nly comfort fraught!
What e'er I do, where'er I be.
Still 'tis God's hand that leadeth me.

He leadeth me, He leadeth me!
By His own hand He leadeth me!
His faithful follow'r I would be,
For by His hand He leadeth me.
—*Joseph H. Gilmore*

O God, beneath Thy Guiding Hand

O God, beneath Thy guiding hand
Our exiled fathers crossed the sea;
And when they trod the wintry strand,
With pray'r and psalm they worshipped Thee.
—*Leonard Bacon*

Trust and Obey

When we walk with the Lord
In the light of His Word,
What a glory He sheds on our way!
While we do His good will
He abides with us still,
And with all who will trust and obey.

Trust and obey—
For there's no other way
To be happy in Jesus
But to trust and obey.

—John Sammis

O That the Lord Would Guide My Ways

O that the Lord would guide my ways,
To keep His statutes still!
Oh that my God would grant me grace,
To know and do His will!

Make me walk in Thy commands;
'Tis a delightful road;
Nor let my head or heart or hands,
Offend against my God.

—Isaac Watts

The LORD is near to

all who call on him,

to all who call on him in truth.

He fulfills the desires

of those who fear him;

he hears their cry and saves them.

Psalm 145:18–19

WORSHIP

Bill of Rights

Congress shall make no law respecting an establishment of religion, or prohibiting the free exercise thereof; or abridging the freedom of speech, or of the press; or the right of the people peaceably to assemble, and to petition the Government for a redress of grievances.

First Amendment
Approved December 15, 1791

Scriptures about Holiness

So you will be my people,
   and I will be your God.

—Jeremiah 30:22

Know that the LORD is God.
   It is he who made us, and we are his;
   we are his people, the sheep of his pasture.

—Psalm 100:3

If anyone obeys his word, God's love is truly made complete in him. This is how we know we are in him: Whoever claims to live in him must walk as Jesus did. *—1 John 2:5–6*

Blessed are they who keep his statutes
   and seek him with all their heart.

—Psalm 119:2

Let us examine our ways and test them,
   and let us return to the LORD.

—Lamentations 3:40

Christ died for our sins according to the Scriptures.
—1 Corinthians 15:3

Help us, O God our Savior,
    for the glory of your name;
deliver us and forgive our sins
    for your name's sake.
Why should the nations say,
    "Where is their God?"

—Psalm 79:9–10

When we were overwhelmed by sins,
    you forgave our transgressions.

—Psalm 65:3

" I will cleanse them from all the sin they have
committed against me and will forgive all their sins
of rebellion against me. Then this city will bring
me renown, joy, praise and honor before all
nations on earth that hear of all the good things I
do for it; and they will be in awe and will tremble
at the abundant prosperity and peace I provide
for it."   *—Jeremiah 33:8–9*

" And so I will show my greatness and my holiness,
and I will make myself known in the sight of many
nations. Then they will know that I am the LORD."

—Ezekiel 38:23

Put on the new self, created to be like God in true
righteousness and holiness.   *—Ephesians 4:24*

But just as he who called you is holy, so be holy in
all you do; for it is written: "Be holy, because I am
holy."   *—1 Peter 1:15–16*

But now that you have been set free from sin and
have become slaves to God, the benefit you reap
leads to holiness, and the result is eternal life.
                                     —Romans 6:22

Since we have these promises, dear friends, let us
purify ourselves from everything that contaminates
body and spirit, perfecting holiness out of
reverence for God.   *—2 Corinthians 7:1*

Make every effort to live in peace with all men and
to be holy; without holiness no one will see the
Lord.   *—Hebrews 12:14*

For God did not call us to be impure, but to live a
holy life.   *—1 Thessalonians 4:7*

Scriptures about Repentance

The Lord is not slow in keeping his promise, as some understand slowness. He is patient with you, not wanting anyone to perish, but everyone to come to repentance.　　　　　　　*−2 Peter 3:9*

"Even now," declares the LORD,
　　"return to me will all your heart,
　　with fasting and weeping and mourning."
Rend your heart
　　and not your garments.
Return to the LORD your God,
　　for he is gracious and compassionate,
slow to anger and abounding in love,
　　and he relents from sending calamity.
　　　　　　　　　　　　−Joel 2:12−13

Unless the LORD builds the house,
　　its builders labor in vain.
Unless the LORD watches over the city,
　　the watchmen stand guard in vain.
　　　　　　　　　　　　−Psalm 127:1

I seek you with all my heart;
　　do not let me stray from your commands.
　　　　　　　　　　　　−Psalm 119:10

This is what the Sovereign LORD, the Holy One
   of Israel, says:
"In repentance and rest is your salvation,
   in quietness and trust is your strength."
                                    —Isaiah 30:15

In the past God overlooked such ignorance, but
now he commands all people everywhere to
repent. For he has set a day when he will judge the
world with justice by the man he has appointed.
                                    —Acts 17:30–31

John came, baptizing in the desert region and
preaching a baptism of repentance for the forgiveness of sins.   *—Mark 1:4*

This is what the LORD says:
"If you repent, I will restore you
   that you may serve me;
if you utter worthy, not worthless, words,
   you will be my spokesman.
Let this people turn to you."

                                    —Jeremiah 15:19

From one man he made every nation of men, that they should inhabit the whole earth; and he determined the times set for them and the exact places where they should live. God did this so that men would seek him and perhaps reach out for him and find him, though he is not far from each one of us.   —*Acts 17:26–27*

If we confess our sins, he is faithful and just and will forgive us our sins and purify us from all unrighteousness.   —*1 John 1:9*

Let us examine our ways and test them,
    and let us return to the LORD.
                    —*Lamentations 3:40*

I have declared to both Jews and Greeks that they must turn to God in repentance and have faith in our Lord Jesus.   —*Acts 20:21*

For the sake of your name, O LORD,
    forgive my iniquity, though it is great.
                    —*Psalm 25:11*

Restore me, and I will return,
  because you are the LORD my God.

—Jeremiah 31:18

You forgave the iniquity of your people
  and covered all their sins.

—Psalm 85:2

Take words with you
  and return to the LORD.
Say to him:
  "Forgive all our sins
and receive us graciously,
  that we may offer the fruit of our lips."

—Hosea 14:2

Jesus answered them, "It is not the healthy who
need a doctor, but the sick. I have not come to call
the righteous, but sinners to repentance."

—Luke 5:31–32

Each of us will give an account of himself to God.

—Romans 14:12

Scriptures about Grace

"For God so loved the world that he gave his one and only Son, that whoever believes in him shall not perish but have eternal life." *–John 3:16*

For it is by grace you have been saved, through faith—and this not from yourselves, it is the gift of God. *–Ephesians 2:8*

He provided redemption for his people;
    he ordained his covenant forever—
    holy and awesome is his name.

–Psalm 111:9

"Blessed are they
    whose transgressions are forgiven,
    whose sins are covered.
Blessed is the man
    whose sin the Lord will never count
        against him.

–Romans 4:7–8

"For the Son of Man came to seek and to save what was lost." *–Luke 19:10*

"Praise be to the Lord, the God of Israel,
    because he has come and has redeemed
        his people."

–Luke 1:68

"Ask and it will be given to you; seek and you will find; knock and the door will be opened to you. For everyone who asks receives; he who seeks finds; and to him who knocks, the door will be opened."
—Matthew 7:7–8

Let us fix our eyes on Jesus, the author and perfecter of our faith, who for the joy set before him endured the cross, scorning its shame, and sat down at the right hand of the throne of God.
—Hebrews 12:2

In him we have redemption through his blood, the forgiveness of sins, in accordance with the riches of God's grace that he lavished on us with all wisdom and understanding.
—Ephesians 1:7–8

And God is able to make all grace abound to you, so that in all things at all times, having all that you need, you will abound in every good work.
—2 Corinthians 9:8

But to each one of us grace has been given as Christ apportioned it.
—Ephesians 4:7

"My grace is sufficient for you, for my power is made perfect in weakness."
—2 Corinthians 12:9

Scriptures about Healing

Jesus answered them, "It is not the healthy who need a doctor, but the sick. I have not come to call the righteous, but sinners to repentance."

–Luke 5:31–32

Restore me, and I will return,
   because you are the LORD my God.

–Jeremiah 31:18

The angel showed me the river of the water of life, as clear as crystal, flowing from the throne of God and of the Lamb down the middle of the great street of the city. On each side of the river stood the tree of life, bearing twelve crops of fruit, yielding its fruit every month. And the leaves of the tree are for the healing of the nations. No longer will there be any curse. The throne of God and of the Lamb will be in the city, and his servants will serve him. They will see his face, and his name will be on their foreheads. There will be no more night. They will not need the light of a lamp or the light of the sun, for the Lord God will give them light. And they will reign for ever and ever.

–Revelation 22:1–5

I said, "O LORD, have mercy on me;
    heal me, for I have sinned against you."

—*Psalm 41:4*

O LORD my God, I called to you for help
    and you healed me.

—*Psalm 30:2*

Go back and tell Hezekiah, the leader of my
people, "This is what the LORD, the God of your
father David, says: I have heard your prayer and
seen your tears; I will heal you."   —*2 Kings 20:5*

He heals the brokenhearted
    and binds up their wounds.

—*Psalm 147:3*

He welcomed them and spoke to them about the
kingdom of God, and healed those who needed
healing.   —*Luke 9:11*

I will bring health and healing to it; I will heal my
people and will let them enjoy abundant peace and
security.   —*Jeremiah 33:6*

Scriptures about
HEALING

He sent forth his word and healed them;
    he rescued them from the grave.

—Psalm 107:20

By [Christ's] wounds we are healed.

—Isaiah 53:5

Heal me, O Lord, and I will be healed;
    save me and I will be saved,
    for you are the one I praise.

—Jeremiah 17:14

Make level paths for your feet, so that the lame
may not be disabled, but rather healed.

—Hebrews 12:13

Scriptures about Worship and Revival

Glory in his holy name;
　　let the hearts of those who seek the LORD rejoice.
Look to the LORD and his strength;
　　seek his face always.

−1 Chronicles 16:10−11

May all who seek you
　　rejoice and be glad in you;
may those who love your salvation always say,
　　"Let God be exalted!"

−Psalm 70:4

If from there you seek the LORD your God, you will
find him if you look for him with all your heart
and with all your soul.　　*−Deuteronomy 4:29*

Seek the LORD while he may be found;
　　call on him while he is near.

−Isaiah 55:6

[Jesus] said to his disciples, "The harvest is
plentiful but the workers are few. Ask the Lord of
the harvest, therefore, to send out workers into his
harvest field."　　*−Matthew 9:37−38*

God looks down from heaven
  on the sons of men
to see if there are any who understand,
  any who seek God.

—Psalm 53:2

Return to us, O God Almighty!
  Look down from heaven and see!...
Then we will not turn away from you;
  revive us, and we will call on your name.
Restore us, O LORD God Almighty;
  make your face shine upon us,
  that we may be saved.

—Psalm 80:14, 18–19

You will seek me and find me when you seek me
with all your heart.   *—Jeremiah 29:13*

Those who look to him are radiant;
  their faces are never covered with shame.

—Psalm 34:5

Tell the people: This is what the LORD Almighty
says: "Return to me," declares the LORD Almighty,
"and I will return to you," says the LORD Almighty.

—Zechariah 1:3

I love those who love me,
  and those who seek to find me.

—Proverbs 8:17

Seek first his kingdom and his righteousness, and
all these things will be given to you as well.

—Matthew 6:33

Ascribe to the LORD the glory due his name;
  worship the LORD in the splendor of his holiness.

—Psalm 29:2

All the nations you have made
  will come and worship before you, O Lord;
  they will bring glory to your name.

—Psalm 86:9

Reflections about Worship and Grace

There is nothing but God's grace. We walk upon it; we breathe it; we live and die by it.

—Robert Louis Stevenson

If I am not in a state of grace, God bring me there; if I am, God keep me there!   *—Joan of Arc*

All below is strength, and all above is grace.

—John Dryden

The higher a man is in grace, the lower he will be in his own esteem.   *—Charles Haddon Spurgeon*

As grace is first from God, so it is continually from him, as much as light is all day long from the sun, as well as at first dawn or at sun-rising.

—Jonathan Edwards

Amazing Grace

Amazing grace—how sweet the sound—
That saved a wretch like me!
I once was lost but now am found,
Was blind but now I see.
'Twas grace that taught my heart to fear,
And grace my fears relieved;
How precious did that grace appear
The hour I first believed!

—John Newton

Reflections about Worship and Religious Freedom

While just government protects all in their religious rites, true religion affords government its surest support.   —*George Washington*

We are faced with the responsibility of either choosing God or denying Him. But God wants America to repent and return to Him, to love Him with all our hearts, and to love one another.

—*James Kennedy*

I am a most unworthy sinner, but I have cried out to the Lord for grace and mercy, and they have covered me completely.   —*Christopher Columbus*

Satan trembles when he sees
The weakest saint upon his knees.

—*William Cowper*

America seeks no earthly empire built on blood and force. No ambition, no temptation, lures her to thought of foreign dominions. The legions which she sends forth are armed, not with the sword, but with the cross. The higher state to which she seeks the allegiance of all mankind is not of human, but of divine origin. She cherishes no purpose save to merit the favor of Almighty God.

—*Calvin Coolidge*

Before all else, we seek, upon our common labor as a nation, the blessings of Almighty God.

—Dwight D. Eisenhower

Above all, I know there is a Supreme Being who rules the affairs of men and whose goodness and mercy have always followed the American people, and I know He will not turn from us now if we humbly and reverently seek His powerful aid.

—Grover Cleveland

God always hears, and He never forgets. His silence does not mean that He is not listening and is not planning. Probably it means that the best time of deliverance has not come yet, and that He is patiently waiting for the moment to arrive when He may prove His love and His power.

—Mrs. Charles Cowman

True repentance is to cease from sin.

—Saint. Ambrose

You cannot repent too soon, because you do not know how soon it may be too late.

—Thomas Fuller

The Church can have light only as it is full of the Spirit, and it can be full only as the members that compose it are filled individually.   *—A. W. Tozer*

We cannot produce revival, earn revival, or arrange God's timetable of revival visitation. We can only meet God's conditions and seek His face.

—Wesley Duewel

If you are sincerely willing to be restored, reshaped, refreshed and renewed by the Spirit of God, you will begin to discover a dimension of living you've never known before.

—Charles Swindoll

When I seek to point people to Christ, it is because I am convinced that He alone is God's answer to life's deepest problems. I have seen Him bring change in the lives of countless individuals who have turned to Him in true repentance and faith. One of the New Testament's most compelling images of spiritual conversion is found in the phrase *born again* or *new birth*....We need what Jesus was teaching: a spiritual rebirth or renewal from within, by the power of God....It takes place as we turn in faith to Christ and submit ourselves to Him. God Himself takes up residence in our lives through His Holy Spirit.   *—Billy Graham*

Before there can be fullness there must be emptiness. Before God can fill us with Himself we must first be emptied of ourselves.   *—A.W. Tozer*

I urge each man and woman ... to declare before God that you will do your part—to swear by the power of God's indwelling presence that, from this day forward, you will do more to get the Gospel to other people—that you will do more than you've ever done before to speak up for the values and beliefs upon which our nation was founded.
                                                    —James Kennedy

If God's people hunger deeply enough, God will hear and send revival. God requires more than casual prayers for revival. He wants His people to hunger and thirst for His mighty working. To seek God's face is far more than occasionally mentioning revival in our prayer. It involves repeated and prolonged prayer. It requires holy determination in prayer, examining ourselves to see if anything in our lives is hindering God.

—Wesley Duewel

Providing for the free exercise of religion is not just a constitutional mandate; it is a complex and demanding responsibility. *—William Dendinger*

Jesus, Keep Me Near the Cross
Jesus, keep me near the Cross,
There a precious fountain
Free to all—a healing stream,
Flows from Calv'ry's mountain.
In the Cross, in the Cross,
Be my glory ever;
Till my raptured soul shall find
Rest beyond the River.

—Fanny Crosby

My Hope Is Built on Nothing Less

My hope is built on nothing less
Than Jesus' blood and righteousness;
I dare not trust the sweetest frame,
But wholly lean on Jesus' name:
On Christ, the solid rock, I stand;
All other ground is sinking sand.

When He shall come with trumpet sound,
O, may I then in Him be found;
Dress'd in His righteousness alone,
I faultless stand before the throne.
On Christ, the solid rock, I stand;
All other ground is sinking sand.

—*Edward Mote*

Our Country's Voice Is Pleading

Our country's voice is pleading,
Ye men of God arise!
His providence is leading,
The land before you lies;
O'er it the day has brightened,
The promise clothes the soil;
Wide fields for harvest whitened,
Invite the reapers' toil.

—*Maria Frances Anderson*

Onward Christian Soldiers

Onward, Christian Soldiers,
Marching as to war,
With the cross of Jesus
Going on before:
Christ, the Royal Master,
Leads against the foe;
Forward into battle,
See, His banners go.

—*Sabine Baring Gould*

Finally, brothers, whatever is true,

whatever is noble, whatever is right,

whatever is pure, whatever is lovely,

whatever is admirable—if anything

is excellent or praiseworthy—think

about such things.

Philippians 4:8

In God We Trust

In 1864 the Congress of the United States of America approved adding "In God We Trust" to the two-cent coin.

In 1908 legislation was passed and "In God We Trust" was mandatory on all coins.

In 1955 "In God We Trust" became mandatory on all U.S. coins and paper currency.

In 1956 "In God We Trust" became the national motto of the United States.

Scriptures about Honesty

Kings take pleasure in honest lips;
   they value a man who speaks the truth.

—Proverbs 16:13

You must have accurate and honest weights and
measures, so that you may live long in the land the
LORD your God is giving you.   *—Deuteronomy 25:15*

Pray for us. We are sure that we have a clear
conscience and desire to live honorably in every
way.   *—Hebrews 13:18*

An honest answer
   is like a kiss on the lips.

—Proverbs 24:26

The law of the LORD is perfect,
   reviving the soul.
The statutes of the LORD are trustworthy,
   making wise the simple.
The precepts of the LORD are right,
   giving joy to the heart.
The commands of the LORD are radiant,
   giving light to the eyes.

—Psalm 19:7–8

Blessed is the man who fears the LORD,
  who finds great delight in his commands.
—Psalm 112:1

A truthful witness gives honest testimony.
—Proverbs 12:17

His divine power has given us everything we need
for life and godliness through our knowledge of
him who called us by his own glory and goodness.
—2 Peter 1:3

Let your light shine before men, that they may see
your good deeds and praise your Father in heaven.
—Matthew 5:16

Physical training is of some value, but godliness
has value for all things, holding promise for both
the present life and the life to come.
—1 Timothy 4:8

Godliness with contentment is great gain. For we
brought nothing into the world, and we can take
nothing out of it.   *—1 Timothy 6:6–7*

You, man of God, flee from all this, and pursue
righteousness, godliness, faith, love, endurance and
gentleness.   *—1 Timothy 6:11*

Do not follow the crowd in doing wrong. When you give testimony in a lawsuit, do not pervert justice by siding with the crowd, and do not show favoritism to a poor man in his lawsuit.

—Exodus 23:2–3

Blessed are they whose ways are blameless,
  who walk according to the law of the LORD.
Blessed are they who keep his statutes
  and seek him with all their heart.
They do nothing wrong;
  they walk in his ways.
You have laid down precepts
  that are to be fully obeyed.
Oh, that my ways were steadfast
  in obeying your decrees!
Then I would not be put to shame
  when I consider all your commands.
I will praise you with an upright heart
  as I learn your righteous laws.
I will obey your decrees;
  do not utterly forsake me.

—Psalm 119:1–8

Truthful lips endure forever,
  but a lying tongue lasts only a moment.

—Proverbs 12:19

The LORD detests lying lips,
  but he delights in men who are truthful.

—Proverbs 12:22

A truthful witness saves lives,
  but a false witness is deceitful.

—Proverbs 14:25

Now I know that you are a man of God and the
word of the LORD from your mouth is truth.

—I Kings 17:24

Guide me in your truth and teach me,
  for you are God my Savior,
  and my hope is in you all day long.

—Psalm 25:5

Scriptures about Integrity

I know, my God, that you test the heart and are pleased with integrity. All these things have I given willingly and with honest intent. And now I have seen with joy how willingly your people who are here have given to you. *—1 Chronicles 29:17*

The man of integrity walks securely.
—Proverbs 10:9

Humility and the fear of the LORD
bring wealth and honor and life.
—Proverbs 22:4

Do nothing out of selfish ambition or vain conceit, but in humility consider others better than yourselves. Each of you should look not only to your own interests, but also to the interests of others.
—Philippians 2:3–4

Blessed is he who has regard for the weak;
the LORD delivers him in times of trouble.
—Psalm 41:1

He who pursues righteousness and love
finds life, prosperity and honor.
—Proverbs 21:21

Judge me, O LORD, according to my righteousness,
   according to my integrity, O Most High.

—*Psalm 7:8*

May integrity and uprightness protect me,
   because my hope is in you.

—*Psalm 25:21*

From everyone who has been given much, much
will be demanded; and from the one who has been
entrusted with much, much more will be asked.

—*Luke 12:48*

In my integrity you uphold me
   and set me in your presence forever.

—*Psalm 41:12*

Let us not become weary in doing good, for at the
proper time we will reap a harvest if we do not give
up. Therefore, as we have opportunity, let us do
good to all people, especially to those who belong
to the family of believers.   —*Galatians 6:9–10*

Blessed is he whose help is the God of Jacob,
   whose hope is in the LORD his God,
the Maker of heaven and earth,
   the sea, and everything in them—
   the LORD, who remains faithful forever.

—*Psalm 146:5–6*

The integrity of the upright guides them.

–Proverbs 11:3

Righteousness guards the man of integrity.

–Proverbs 13:6

Blessed are the people of whom this is true;
blessed are the people whose God is the LORD.

–Psalm 144:15

Glory, honor and peace for everyone who does good.

–Romans 2:10

The fear of the LORD teaches a man wisdom,
and humility comes before honor.

–Proverbs 15.33

Scriptures about Generosity

Honor the LORD with your wealth. —*Proverbs 3:9*

Jesus said to his host, "When you give a luncheon or dinner, do not invite your friends, your brothers or relatives, or your rich neighbors; if you do, they may invite you back and so you will be repaid. But when you give a banquet, invite the poor, the crippled, the lame, the blind, and you will be blessed. Although they cannot repay you, you will be repaid at the resurrection of the righteous."

—Luke 14:12–14

Love your enemies, do good to those who hate you, bless those who curse you, pray for those who mistreat you. If someone strikes you on one cheek, turn to him the other also. If someone takes your cloak, do not stop him from taking your tunic. Give to everyone who asks you, and if anyone takes what belongs to you, do not demand it back. Do to others as you would have them do to you.

If you love those who love you, what credit is that to you? Even "sinners" love those who love them. And if you do good to those who are good to you, what credit is that to you? Even "sinners" do that. And if you lend to those from whom you expect repayment, what credit is that to you? Even

"sinners" lend to "sinners," expecting to be repaid
in full.   *—Luke 6:27–34*

Keep your lives free from the love of money and be
content with what you have.   *—Hebrews 13:5*

No servant can serve two masters. Either he will
hate the one and love the other, or he will be
devoted to the one and despise the other. You
cannot serve both God and Money.   *—Luke 16:13*

Give, and it will be given to you. A good measure,
pressed down, shaken together and running over,
will be poured into your lap. For with the measure
you use, it will be measured to you.   *—Luke 6:38*

Sell your possessions and give to the poor. Provide
purses for yourselves that will not wear out, a
treasure in heaven that will not be exhausted,
where no thief comes near and no moth destroys.
For where your treasure is, there your heart will be
also.   *—Luke 12:33–34*

Do not go over your vineyard a second time or
pick up the grapes that have fallen. Leave them for
the poor and the alien. I am the LORD your God.
                                            —Leviticus 19:10

Jesus replied: " 'Love the Lord your God with all your heart and with all your soul and with all your mind.' This is the first and greatest commandment. And the second is like it: 'Love your neighbor as yourself.' All the Law and the Prophets hang on these two commandments."   *–Matthew 22:37–40*

Remember this: Whoever sows sparingly will also reap sparingly, and whoever sows generously will also reap generously. Each man should give what he has decided in his heart to give, not reluctantly or under compulsion, for God loves a cheerful giver. And God is able to make all grace abound to you, so that in all things at all times, having all that you need, you will abound in every good work. As it is written:

> "He has scattered abroad his gifts to the poor;
> his righteousness endures forever."

Now he who supplies seed to the sower and bread for food will also supply and increase your store of seed and will enlarge the harvest of your righteousness. You will be made rich in every way so that you can be generous on every occasion, and through us your generosity will result in thanksgiving to God. This service that you perform is not only supplying the needs of God's people but is also overflowing in many expressions of thanks to

God. Because of the service by which you have proved yourselves, men will praise God for the obedience that accompanies your confession of the gospel of Christ, and for your generosity in sharing with them and with everyone else. And in their prayers for you their hearts will go out to you, because of the surpassing grace God has given you. Thanks be to God for his indescribable gift!

–2 Corinthians 9:6–15

I was young and now I am old,
    yet I have never seen the righteous forsaken
    or their children begging bread.
They are always generous and lend freely;
    their children will be blessed.

–Psalm 37:25–26

If there is a poor man among your brothers in any of the towns of the land that the LORD your God is giving you, do not be hardhearted or tightfisted toward your poor brother. Rather be openhanded and freely lend him whatever he needs.

–Deuteronomy 15:7–8

Do not take advantage of a hired man who is poor and needy, whether he is a brother Israelite or an alien living in one of your towns. Pay him his wages each day before sunset, because he is poor

and is counting on it. Otherwise he may cry to the
LORD against you, and you will be guilty of sin.

—Deuteronomy 24:14–15

Good will come to him who is generous and
    lends freely,
  who conducts his affairs with justice.
Surely he will never be shaken;
  a righteous man will be remembered forever.
He will have no fear of bad news;
  his heart is steadfast, trusting in the LORD.
His heart is secure, he will have no fear;
  in the end he will look in triumph on his foes.
He has scattered abroad his gifts to the poor,
  his righteousness endures forever;
  his horn will be lifted high in honor.

—Psalm 112:5–9

Reflections about Stewardship

I hope I shall always possess firmness and virtue
enough to maintain what I consider the most
enviable of all titles, the character of an "Honest
Man."
—George Washington

If we abide by the principles taught in the Bible,
our country will go on prospering and to prosper;
but if we and our posterity neglect its instructions
and authority, no man can tell how sudden a
catastrophe may overwhelm us and bury all our
glory in profound obscurity.   *—Daniel Webster*

I summon all honest men, all patriotic, all forward-
looking men, to my side. God helping me, I will not
fail them, if they will but counsel and sustain me!
—Woodrow Wilson

I deem the present occasion sufficiently important
and solemn to justify me in expressing to my
fellow-citizens a profound reverence for the
Christian religion and a thorough conviction that
sound morals, religious liberty, and a just sense of
religious responsibility are essentially connected
with all true and lasting happiness.
—William Henry Harrison

An honest man is the noblest work of God.
                                    —Alexander Pope

For we must consider that we shall be as a City upon a hill. The eyes of all people are upon us. So that if we shall deal falsely with our God in this work we have undertaken and so cause him to withdraw his present help from us, we shall be made a story and a byword throughout the world.
                                    —John Winthrop

If you want to be respected for your actions, then your behavior must be above reproach. If our lives demonstrate that we are peaceful, humble, and trusted, this is recognized by others.   *—Rosa Parks*

I know now what the task means. I realize to the full the responsibility which it involves. I pray God I may be given the wisdom and the prudence to do my duty in the true spirit of this great people.
                                    —Woodrow Wilson

America's record in this century has been unparalleled in the world's history for its responsibility, for its generosity, for its creativity, and for its progress.   *—Richard Nixon*

If I felt that there is to be sole responsibility in the Executive for the America of tomorrow I should shrink from the burden. But here are a hundred millions, with common concern and shared responsibility, answerable to God and country.

—Warren Harding

In the presence of my countrymen, mindful of the solemnity of this occasion, knowing what the task means and the responsibility which it involves, I beg your tolerance, your aid, and your cooperation. I ask the help of Almighty God in this service to my country to which you have called me.

—Herbert Hoover

In the submission
to God's will
and the laws of nature,
may be found
the tranquillity of mind
that brings peace
and contentment,
as the night comes on.

—Benjamin Franklin

It must be a government which submits loyally and heartily to the Constitution and the laws—the laws of the nation and the laws of the States themselves—accepting and obeying faithfully the whole Constitution as it is. Resting upon this sure and substantial foundation, the superstructure of beneficent local governments can be built up, and not otherwise.   *—Rutherford B. Hayes*

God gives us biblical principles not so that we can arrange our lives according to our taste, but so that we can know how God wants us to live.

—Larry Crabb

He that sees the beauty of holiness, or true moral good, sees the greatest and most important thing in the world.... Unless this is seen, nothing is seen that is worth seeing; for there is no other true excellence or beauty.   *—Jonathan Edwards*

Do you wish to be great? Then begin by being. Do you desire to construct a vast and lofty fabric? Think first about the foundations of humility. The higher your structure is to be, the deeper must be its foundation.   *—St. Augustine*

There is no true holiness without humility.
> *—Thomas Fuller*

It is a great deal better to live a holy life than to talk about it. Lighthouses do not ring bells and fire cannon to call attention to their shining—they just shine.
> *—Dwight D. Moody*

It is through the power of his Spirit in us that we can walk in holiness.
> *—Jack Deere*

The serene, silent beauty of a holy life is the most powerful influence in the world, next to the might of the Spirit of God.
> *—Blaise Pascal*

This is what the LORD Almighty says: "Administer true justice; show mercy and compassion to one another."

Zechariah 7:9

JUSTICE

The Original Pledge of Allegiance

I pledge allegiance to my Flag,
and the Republic for which it stands,
one nation indivisible—with liberty
and justice for all.

Francis Bellamy, 1892

At the first National Flag Conference in Washington D.C., on June 14, 1923, a change was made for clarity: the words "the Flag of the United States" replaced "my flag."

In 1942 Congress officially recognized the Pledge of Allegiance.

In June of 1954 an amendment was made to add the words "under God." President Dwight D. Eisenhower said, "In this way we are reaffirming the transcendence of religious faith in America's heritage and future; in this way we shall constantly strengthen those spiritual weapons which forever will be our country's most powerful resource in peace and war."

The Pledge of Allegiance

I pledge allegiance to the flag

of the United States of America.

And to the republic for which it stands,

one nation, under God, indivisible.

With liberty and justice for all.

Scriptures about Justice

By justice a king gives a country stability.

—Proverbs 29:4

My eyes will be on the faithful in the land,
    that they may dwell with me;
he whose walk is blameless
    will minister to me.

—Psalm 101:6

This is what Hezekiah did throughout Judah,
doing what was good and right and faithful before
the LORD his God. In everything that he undertook
in the service of God's temple and in obedience to
the law and the commands, he sought his God and
worked wholeheartedly. And so he prospered.

—2 Chronicles 31:20–21

Appoint judges and officials for each of your tribes
in every town the LORD your God is giving you, and
they shall judge the people fairly. Follow justice
and justice alone, so that you may live and possess
the land the LORD your God is giving you.

—Deuteronomy 16:18, 20

And you, Ezra, in accordance with the wisdom of
your God, which you possess, appoint magistrates
and judges to administer justice to all the people.

—Ezra 7:25

But you must return to your God;
  maintain love and justice,
  and wait for your God always.

—Hosea 12:6

For the LORD is righteous,
  he loves justice;
  upright men will see his face.

—Psalm 11:7

Let love and faithfulness never leave you;
  bind them around your neck,
  write them on the tablet of your heart.
Then you will win favor and a good name
  in the sight of God and man.

—Proverbs 3:3–4

Love and faithfulness keep a king safe;
  through love his throne is made secure.

—Proverbs 20:28

Here is my servant, whom I uphold,
  my chosen one in whom I delight;
I will put my Spirit on him
  and he will bring justice to the nations.

—Isaiah 42:1

Blessed are they who maintain justice,
  who constantly do what is right.

—Psalm 106:3

Good will come to him who is generous and lends
    freely,
  who conducts his affairs with justice.

—Psalm 112:5

I put on righteousness as my clothing;
  justice was my robe and my turban.

—Job 29:14

Let justice roll on like a river,
  righteousness like a never-failing stream!

—Amos 5:24

The LORD loves righteousness and justice;
  the earth is full of his unfailing love.

—Psalm 33:5

Scripture about

JUSTICE

Your throne, O God, will last for ever and ever;
  a scepter of justice will be the scepter of your
    kingdom.

—Psalm 45:6

The King is mighty, he loves justice—
  you have established equity;
in Jacob you have done
  what is just and right.

—Psalm 99:4

The righteous care about justice for the poor.

—Proverbs 29:7

See, a king will reign in righteousness
  and rulers will rule with justice.

—Isaiah 32:1

If you know that [God] is righteous, you know that
everyone who does what is right has been born of
him.   —1 John 2:29

Speak and act as those who are going to be judged
by the law that gives freedom, because judgment
without mercy will be shown to anyone who has
not been merciful. Mercy triumphs over judgment!

—James 2:12–13

Scriptures about
JUSTICE

Test me, O LORD, and try me,
    examine my heart and my mind;
for your love is ever before me,
    and I walk continually in your truth.

—Psalm 26:2–3

The LORD loves the just
    and will not forsake his faithful ones.

—Psalm 37:28

Blessed are those who dwell in your house;
    they are ever praising you.
Blessed are those whose strength is in you,
    who have set their hearts on pilgrimage.

—Psalm 84:4–5

A man's wisdom gives him patience;
    it is to his glory to overlook an offense.

—Proverbs 19:11

Scriptures about Understanding

For wisdom is more precious than rubies,
   and nothing you desire can compare with her.
"I, wisdom, dwell together with prudence;
   I possess knowledge and discretion.
Counsel and sound judgment are mine;
   I have understanding and power.
By me kings reign
   and rulers make laws that are just;
by me princes govern,
   and all nobles who rule on earth.
I love those who love me,
   and those who seek me find me."

—Proverbs 8:11–12, 14–17

Show me your ways, O LORD,
   teach me your paths;
guide me in your truth and teach me,
   for you are God my Savior,
   and my hope is in you all day long.

—Psalm 25:4–5

And this is my prayer: that your love may abound
more and more in knowledge and depth of insight,
so that you may be able to discern what is best and
may be pure and blameless until the day of Christ.

—Philippians 1:9–10

We have not stopped praying for you and asking
God to fill you with the knowledge of his will
through all spiritual wisdom and understanding.
And we pray this in order that you may live a life
worthy of the Lord and may please him in every
way: bearing fruit in every good work, growing in
the knowledge of God, being strengthened with all
power according to his glorious might so that you
may have great endurance and patience, and
joyfully giving thanks to the Father.

—Colossians 1:9–12

O Lord, since you are my rock and my fortress,
    for the sake of your name lead and guide me.

—Psalm 31:3

Lead me, O LORD, in your righteousness
    because of my enemies—
    make straight your way before me.

—Psalm 5:8

The fear of the LORD is the beginning of wisdom;
    all who follow his precepts have good
        understanding.
    To him belongs eternal praise.

—Psalm 111:10

Blessed is the man who finds wisdom,
the man who gains understanding.

—Proverbs 3:13

Do not forsake wisdom, and she will protect you;
love her, and she will watch over you.
Wisdom is supreme; therefore get wisdom.
Though it cost all you have, get understanding.

—Proverbs 4:6–7

The Spirit of the LORD will rest on him—
the Spirit of wisdom and of understanding,
the Spirit of counsel and of power,
the Spirit of knowledge and of the fear
of the LORD.

—Isaiah 11:2

Who endowed the heart with wisdom
or gave understanding to the mind?

—Job 38:36

The LORD gives wisdom,
and from his mouth comes knowledge and
understanding.

—Proverbs 2:6

But the wisdom that comes from heaven is first of all pure; then peace-loving, considerate, submissive, full of mercy and good fruit, impartial and sincere.

—James 3:17

O LORD, you have searched me
    and you know me.
You know when I sit and when I rise;
    you perceive my thoughts from afar.
You discern my going out and my lying down;
    you are familiar with all my ways.
Before a word is on my tongue
    you know it completely, O LORD.
You hem me in—behind and before;
    you have laid your hand upon me.
Such knowledge is too wonderful for me,
    too lofty for me to attain.
Where can I go from your Spirit?
    Where can I flee from your presence?
If I go up to the heavens, you are there;
    if I make my bed in the depths, you are there.
If I rise on the wings of the dawn,
    if I settle on the far side of the sea,
even there your hand will guide me,
    your right hand will hold me fast.

—Psalm 139:1–10

Scriptures about Righteousness

Blessings crown the head of the righteous.

—Proverbs 10:6

He who pursues righteousness and love
   finds life, prosperity and honor.

—Proverbs 21:21

The fruit of righteousness will be peace;
   the effect of righteousness will be quietness and
   confidence forever.

—Isaiah 32:17

Therefore confess your sins to each other and pray
for each other so that you may be healed. The
prayer of a righteous man is powerful and effective.

—James 5:16

The mouth of the righteous man utters wisdom,
   and his tongue speaks what is just.
The law of his God is in his heart;
   his feet do not slip.

—Psalm 37:30–31

I walk in the way of righeousness,
   along the paths of justice.

—Proverbs 8:20

The LORD rewards every man for his righteousness
and faithfulness.   *—1 Samuel 26:23*

The LORD detests the way of the wicked
   but he loves those who pursue righteousness.
                       —Proverbs 15:9

The righteous man leads a blameless life;
   blessed are his children after him.
                       Proverbs 20:7

Your statutes are my heritage forever;
   they are the joy of my heart.
                       —Psalm 119:111

Tell the righteous it will be well with them,
   for they will enjoy the fruit of their deeds.
                       Isaiah 3:10

For the eyes of the Lord are on the righteous
   and his ears are attentive to their prayer . . .
                       —1 Peter 3:12

The law of the LORD is perfect, reviving the soul.
                       —Psalm 19:7

Righteousness exalts a nation . . .

                       —Proverbs 14:34

Scriptures about Honor

Glory, honor and peace for everyone who does good: first for the Jew, then for the Gentile.

—Romans 2:10

Show proper respect to everyone: Love the brother-hood of believers, fear God, honor the king.

—1 Peter 2:17

My salvation and my honor depend on God;
  he is my mighty rock, my refuge.

—Psalm 62:7

He will call upon me, and I will answer him;
  I will be with him in trouble,
  I will deliver him and honor him.

—Psalm 91:15

He has declared that he will set you in praise, fame and honor high above all the nations he has made and that you will be a people holy to the LORD your God, as he promised.   *—Deuteronomy 26:19*

It is to a man's honor to avoid strife.

—Proverbs 20:3

Scriptures about
HONOR

For the LORD God is a sun and shield;
   the LORD bestows favor and honor;
no good thing does he withhold
   from those whose walk is blameless.
                                    —Psalm 84:11

He will make your righteousness shine like
   the dawn,
   the justice of your cause like the noonday sun.
                                    —Psalm 37:6

Now to the King eternal, immortal, invisible, the
only God, be honor and glory for ever and ever.
Amen.   *—1 Timothy 1:17*

Just as the Father raises the dead and gives them
life, even so the Son gives life to whom he is
pleased to give it. Moreover, the Father judges no
one, but has entrusted all judgment to the Son, that
all may honor the Son just as they honor the
Father. He who does not honor the Son does not
honor the Father, who sent him.   *—John 5:21–23*

Reflections about Justice

May we, in our dealings with all peoples of the earth, ever speak truth and serve justice.

—Dwight D. Eisenhower

Equal and exact justice to all men, of whatever state or persuasion, religious or political; peace, commerce, and honest friendship with all nations.

—Thomas Jefferson

Justice cannot be for one side alone, but must be for both.   *—Eleanor Roosevelt*

All virtue is summed up in dealing justly.

—Aristotle

It has been the true glory of the United States to cultivate peace by observing justice.

—James Madison

God has placed upon our head a diadem and has laid at our feet power and wealth beyond definition or calculation. But we must not forget that we take these gifts upon the condition that justice and mercy shall hold the reins of power and that the upward avenues of hope shall be free to all the people.   *—Benjamin Harrison*

Reflections about
JUSTICE

With God's help, the future of mankind will be assured in a world of justice, harmony, and peace.
—*Harry S. Truman*

The feelings with which we face this new age of right and opportunity sweep across our heartstrings like some air out of God's own presence, where justice and mercy are reconciled and the judge and the brother are one. —*Woodrow Wilson*

We believe that all men have a right to equal justice under law and equal opportunity to share in the common good. —*Harry S. Truman*

There must be justice, sensed and shared by all peoples, for without justice the world can know only a tense and unstable truce.
—*Dwight D. Eisenhower*

Justice delayed is democracy denied.
—*Robert F. Kennedy*

Justice is the great interest of man on earth.
—*Daniel Webster*

If we expect others to rely on our fairness and justice we must show that we rely on their fairness and justice. —*Calvin Coolidge*

I shall greatly rely upon the wisdom and patriotism of Congress and of those who may share with me the responsibilities and duties of administration.

—James A. Garfield

After all, the Constitution reserves for Congress the right to advise and consent. As I see it, the Founding Fathers intended to follow the biblical precept that in the counsel of many there is wisdom.

—Oliver North

For myself, I ask only, in the words of an ancient leader: "Give me now wisdom and knowledge, that I may go out and come in before this people: for who can judge this thy people, that is so great?"

—Lyndon Baines Johnson

I shall need, too, the favor of that Being in whose hands we are, who led our fathers, as Israel of old, from their native land and planted them in a country flowing with all the necessaries and comforts of life; who has covered our infancy with His providence and our riper years with His wisdom and power.

—Thomas Jefferson

Let not the foundation of our hope rest upon man's wisdom.... It must be felt that there is no national security but in the nation's humble, acknowledged dependence upon God and His overruling providence.
—Franklin Pierce

I accept with humility the honor which the American people have conferred upon me. I accept it with a deep resolve to do all that I can for the welfare of this Nation and for the peace of the world.
—Harry S. Truman

I join in the hope that when my time as your President has ended, people might say this about our Nation: that we had remembered the words of Micah and renewed our search for humility, mercy, and justice.
—Jimmy Carter

I accept my part with single-mindedness of purpose and humility of spirit, and implore the favor and guidance of God in His Heaven.
—Warren G. Harding

All below is strength, and all above is grace.
—John Dryden

The times demand big men. Not men who are big shots, but men who are big in heart and mind. Great men! Large-souled men!

—Richard Halverson

Aristotle defined character as the decisions a person makes when the choice is not obvious. My father used to say, "Character is the way we act when nobody's looking." *—D. Bruce Lockerbie*

God gives to every man virtue, temper, and understanding. *—William Cowper*

A Christian man is the most free lord of all, and subject to none; a Christian man is the most dutiful servant of all, and subject to everyone.

—Martin Luther

The study of God's word, for the purpose of discovering God's will, is the secret discipline which has formed the greatest characters.

—James W. Alexander

COMMUNITY

The Statue of Liberty

Give me your tired, your poor,
Your huddled masses
yearning to breathe free,
The wretched refuse
of your teeming shore.
Send these, the homeless,
tempest-tossed to me.
I lift my lamp beside the golden door.

Emma Lazarus, 1903

COMMUNITY

The Gettysburg Address

*Four score and seven years ago our fathers
brought forth on this continent, a new nation,
conceived in liberty, and dedicated to the
proposition that all men are created equal....
That this nation, under God, shall have a
new birth of freedom—and that government
of the people, by the people, for the people,
shall not perish from the earth.*

Abraham Lincoln
November 19, 1863

Scriptures about Community

The body is a unit, though it is made up of many parts; and though all its parts are many, they form one body. So it is with Christ. For we were all baptized by one Spirit into one body—whether Jews or Greeks, slave or free—and we were all given the one Spirit to drink.   *—1 Corinthians 12:12–13*

How good and pleasant it is
    when brothers live together in unity!
                                —Psalm 133:1

Be devoted to one another in brotherly love.
Honor one another above yourselves.
                                —Romans 12:10

Do to others as you would have them do to you.
                                —Luke 6:31

Whoever loves his brother lives in the light, and there is nothing in him to make him stumble.
                                —1 John 2:10

Scriptures about
COMMUNITY

Make every effort to add to your faith goodness; and to goodness, knowledge; and to knowledge, self-control; and to self-control, perseverance; and to perseverance, godliness; and to godliness, brotherly kindness; and to brotherly kindness, love.   *—2 Peter 1:5–7*

Therefore, as God's chosen people, holy and dearly loved, clothe yourselves with compassion, kindness, humility, gentleness and patience. Bear with each other and forgive whatever grievances you may have against one another. Forgive as the Lord forgave you. And over all these virtues put on love, which binds them all together in perfect unity.
                              —Colossians 3:12–14

Dear friends, let us love one another, for love comes from God. Everyone who loves has been born of God and knows God. And he has given us this command: Whoever loves God must also love his brother.   *—1 John 4:7, 21*

How great is the love the Father has lavished on us, that we should be called children of God! And that is what we are!   *—1 John 3:1*

Scriptures about Peace

If it is possible, as far as it depends on you, live at peace with everyone.   *—Romans 12:18*

Blessed are the peacemakers,
   for they will be called sons of God.
                              —Matthew 5:9

Peacemakers who sow in peace raise a harvest of righteousness.   *—James 3:18*

" I will grant peace in the land, and you will lie down and no one will make you afraid."
                              —Leviticus 26:6

But the meek will inherit the land
   and enjoy great peace.
                              —Psalm 37:11

The LORD gives strength to his people;
   the LORD blesses his people with peace.
                              —Psalm 29:11

Aim for perfection, listen to my appeal, be of one mind, live in peace. And the God of love and peace will be with you.   *—2 Corinthians 13:11*

Scriptures about
PEACE

Let the peace of Christ rule in your hearts, since as members of one body you were called to peace.

—Colossians 3:15

LORD, you establish peace for us;
all that we have accomplished you have done for us.

—Isaiah 26:12

God is not a God of disorder but of peace.

—1 Corinthians 14:33

If only you had paid attention to my commands,
your peace would have been like a river,
your righteousness like the waves of the sea.

—Isaiah 48:18

This is what the LORD says:
"I will extend peace to her like a river,
and the wealth of nations like a flooding stream."

—Isaiah 66:12

I will make a covenant of peace with them; it will be an everlasting covenant. I will establish them and increase their numbers, and I will put my sanctuary among them forever. My dwelling place will be with them; I will be their God, and they will be my people.

—Ezekiel 37:26–27

Peace I leave with you; my peace I give you. I do not give to you as the world gives. Do not let your hearts be troubled and do not be afraid.

—John 14:27

My covenant was with him, a covenant of life and peace, and I gave them to him; this called for reverence and he revered me and stood in awe of my name. True instruction was in his mouth and nothing false was found on his lips. He walked with me in peace and uprightness, and turned many from sin.   *—Malachi 2:5–6*

You will keep in perfect peace
   him whose mind is steadfast,
   because he trusts in you.

—Isaiah 26:3

A heart at peace gives life to the body.

—Proverbs 14:30

When a man's ways are pleasing to the LORD,
   he makes even his enemies live at peace with him.

—Proverbs 16:7

The mind controlled by the Spirit is life and peace.

—Romans 8:6

Scriptures about Reconciliation

Go back and tell Hezekiah, the leader of my people, "This is what the LORD, the God of your father David, says: 'I have heard your prayer and seen your tears; I will heal you.'"   *—2 Kings 20:5*

He heals the brokenhearted
and binds up their wounds.

—Psalm 147:3

Submit to God and be at peace with him;
in this way prosperity will come to you.

—Job 22:21

Whatever you have learned or received or heard from me, or seen in me—put it into practice. And the God of peace will be with you.

—Philippians 4:9

For you who revere my name, the sun of righteousness will rise with healing in its wings.

—Malachi 4:2

He welcomed them and spoke to them about the kingdom of God, and healed those who needed healing.   *—Luke 9:11*

I will bring health and healing to it; I will heal my people and will let them enjoy abundant peace and security.
                                                          —Jeremiah 33:6

He himself is our peace, who has made the two one and has destroyed the barrier, the dividing wall of hostility . . . thus making peace, and in this one body to reconcile both of them to God through the cross, by which he put to death their hostility. He came and preached peace to you who were far away and peace to those who were near. For through him we both have access to the Father by one Spirit.
                                                     —Ephesians 2:14–18

I appeal to you, brothers, in the name of our Lord Jesus Christ, that all of you agree with one another so that there may be no divisions among you and that you may be perfectly united in mind and thought.
                                                  —1 Corinthians 1:10

I will listen to what God the LORD will say;
    he promises peace to his people, his saints—
    but let them not return to folly.

                                                        —Psalm 85:8

Scriptures about
RECONCILIATION

There is no difference between Jew and Gentile—
the same Lord is Lord of all and richly blesses all
who call on him.   *—Romans 10:12*

Confess your sins to each other and pray for each
other so that you may be healed. The prayer of a
righteous man is powerful and effective.
                                              —James 5:16

I did not see a temple in the city, because the Lord
God Almighty and the Lamb are its temple. The
city does not need the sun or the moon to shine on
it, for the glory of God gives it light, and the Lamb
is its lamp. The nations will walk by its light, and
the kings of the earth will bring their splendor into
it. On no day will its gates ever be shut, for there
will be no night there. The glory and honor of the
nations will be brought into it.
                                      —Revelation 21:22–26

Reflections about Community

With malice toward none, with charity for all, with firmness in the right as God gives us to see the right, let us strive on to finish the work we are in, to bind up the nation's wounds, to care for him who shall have borne the battle and for his widow and his orphan, to do all which may achieve and cherish a just and lasting peace among ourselves and with all nations. *—Abraham Lincoln*

Our doctrine of equality and liberty and humanity comes from our belief in the brotherhood of man, through the fatherhood of God. *—Calvin Coolidge*

We believe that all men are created equal because they are created in the image of God.
—Harry S. Truman

No race can prosper till it learns that there is as much dignity in tilling a field as in writing a poem.
—Booker T. Washington

The physical configuration of the earth has separated us from all of the Old World, but the common brotherhood of man, the highest law of all our being, has united us by inseparable bonds with all humanity. *—Calvin Coolidge*

America is ready to encourage, eager to initiate, and promote that brotherhood of mankind which must be God's highest conception of human relationship.　　　　　*—Warren G. Harding*

The Bible teaches us that there is no foundation for enduring peace on earth except in righteousness; that it is our duty to suffer for that cause if need be; that we are bound to fight for it if we have the power; and that if God gives us the victory we must use it for the perpetuation of righteous peace.　　　　　*—Henry van Dyke*

Peace, like charity, begins at home.

—Franklin D. Roosevelt

May it be among the dispensations of His providence to bless our beloved country with honors and with length of days. May her ways be ways of pleasantness and all her paths be peace!

—Martin Van Buren

And may that Infinite Power which rules the destinies of the universe lead our councils to what is best, and give them a favorable issue for your peace and prosperity.　　　　　*—Thomas Jefferson*

We ought to cultivate peace, commerce, and friendship with all nations, and this not merely as the best means of promoting our own material interests, but in a spirit of Christian benevolence toward our fellow-men, wherever their lot may be cast.
—James Buchanan

The unselfishness of these United States is a thing proven; our devotion to peace for ourselves and for the world is well established; our concern for preserved civilization has had its impassioned and heroic expression.
—Warren G. Harding

The United States fully accepts the profound truth that our own progress, prosperity, and peace are interlocked with the progress, prosperity, and peace of all humanity.
—Herbert Hoover

Would you have peace with God? . . . the Lord Jesus has shed his heart's blood for this. He died for this; he rose again for this; he ascended into the highest heaven, and is now interceding at the right hand of God.
—George Whitefield

May the turbulence of our age yield to a true time of peace, when men and nations shall share a life that honors the dignity of each, the brotherhood of all.
—Dwight D. Eisenhower

Reflections about
COMMUNITY

There is no solid basis for civilization but in the Word of God. If we abide by the principles taught in the Bible, our country will go on prospering and to prosper. I make it a practice to read the Bible through once every year. —*Daniel Webster*

For more than three centuries, moral values have been the life-support system of this country. The men and women who planted their stand on these shores in the year 1607 vowed to build here a nation founded on virtue and moral integrity. And during all those years their promises and plan held true. The American people brought forth on this continent a nation dedicated to liberty and justice. The founders were committed to strong moral principles based on individual liberty and personal responsibility. —*James Kennedy*

For it isn't enough to talk about peace. One must believe in it. And it isn't enough to believe in it. One must work at it. —*Eleanor Roosevelt*

There is nothing wrong with America that the faith, love of freedom, intelligence and energy of her citizens cannot cure. —*Dwight D. Eisenhower*

I'm calling for individual Christians to become ...
informed citizens who will enter their community ... on social and political issues. If a
religion is really vital, meaningful, relevant, and
important, it will make a difference not only in the
lives of individuals but also in society itself.

—*Bob Briner*

Our ancestors established their system of
government on morality and religious sentiment.
Moral habits, they believed, cannot safely be
trusted on any other foundation than religious
principle, nor any government be secure which is
not supported by moral habits.... Whatever makes
men good Christians, makes them good citizens.

—*Daniel Webster, at the bicentennial celebration*
of the landing of the Pilgrims at Plymouth Rock,
December 22, 1820

As effective as individual Christians can be—and
with God's help one person acting alone can do
mighty things—it is almost always true that acting
in concert we can do even more. When the body of
Christ works in harmony and unison, the most
effective kingdom building is done.

—*Bob Briner*

COMMUNITY

If we remember that God loves us and that we can love others as he loves us, then America can become the sign of peace for the whole world, the sign of joy from where a sign of care for the weakest and the weak, the unborn child, must go out to the world. If you become a burning light of justice and peace in the world, then really you will be true to what the founders of this country stood for. This is to love one another as God loves each one of us. And where does this love begin? In our own home. How does it begin? By praying together.

—*Mother Teresa*

Make us worthy, Lord, to serve our fellow men throughout the world who live and die in poverty and hunger. Give them through our hands this day their daily bread, and by our understanding love, give peace and joy.

Jesus came to give us the good news that God loves us and that he wants us to love one another as he loves each one of us. And to make it easy for us to love one another, Jesus said, "Whatever you do to the least, you do it to me. If you give a glass of water, you give it to me. If you receive a little child in my name, you receive me. So whatever you do to the least, you do it to me."

And where does this love begin? In our own families. How does it begin? By praying together.

The family that prays together stays together, and if you stay together, you will love each other as God loves each one of you. So teach your children to pray, and pray with them, and you will have the joy and the peace and the unity of Christ's own love living in you.
                                                —*Mother Teresa*

We voice our hope and our belief that we can help to heal this divided world.
                                                —*Dwight D. Eisenhower*

The first test of a truly great man is his humility.
                                                —*John Ruskin*

Humility like darkness reveals the heavenly lights.
                                                —*Henry David Thoreau*

The church was and is the foundation of our community. It became our strength, our refuge, and our haven.
                                                —*Rosa Parks*

The foundations of our society and our government rest so much on the teachings of the Bible that it would be difficult to support them if faith in these teachings would cease to be practically universal in our country.
                                                —*Calvin Coolidge*

$\mathcal{S}$ERVICE

Greater love has no one

than this, that he lay down

his life for his friends.

John 15:13

SERVICE

Our Flag: A Symbol of Service

June 14, 1777, the Continental Congress passed the first Flag Act: "Resolved, That the flag of the United States be made of thirteen stripes, alternate red and white; that the union be thirteen stars, white in a blue field, representing a new Constellation."

Act of April 4, 1818, provided for thirteen stripes— representing the thirteen original colonies, and one star for each state, to be added to the flag on the Fourth of July following the admission of each new state, signed by President Monroe.

Scriptures about Faithfulness

Now it is required that those who have been given
a trust must prove faithful.   *−1 Corinthians 4:2*

My eyes will be on the faithful in the land,
    that they may dwell with me;
he whose walk is blameless
    will minister to me.

−Psalm 101:6

His master replied, "Well done, good and faithful
servant! You have been faithful with a few things; I
will put you in charge of many things."

−Matthew 25:21

Jesus was faithful to the one who appointed him,
just as Moses was faithful in all God's house.

−Hebrews 3:2

To the faithful you show yourself faithful.

−2 Samuel 22:26

God, who has called you into fellowship with his
Son Jesus Christ our Lord, is faithful.

−1 Corinthians 1:9

I thank Christ Jesus our Lord, who has given me strength, that he considered me faithful, appointing me to his service. *—1 Timothy 1:12*

It gave me great joy to have some brothers come and tell about your faithfulness to the truth and how you continue to walk in the truth.... Dear friend, you are faithful in what you are doing for the brothers, even though they are strangers to you.

—3 John 3, 5

Know therefore that the LORD your God is God; he is the faithful God, keeping his covenant of love to a thousand generations of those who love him and keep his commands. *—Deuteronomy 7:9*

Let love and faithfulness never leave you;
    bind them around your neck,
    write them on the tablet of your heart.
Then you will win favor and a good name
    in the sight of God and man.

—Proverbs 3:3–4

Love and faithfulness keep a king safe;
    through love his throne is made secure.
—Proverbs 20:28

Scriptures about Accountability

What will I do when God confronts me?
  What will I answer when called to account?
                                        —Job 31:14

They will have to give account to him who is ready
to judge the living and the dead.
                                        —1 Peter 4:5

Do not forsake wisdom, and she will protect you;
  love her, and she will watch over you.
Wisdom is supreme; therefore get wisdom.
  Though it cost all you have, get understanding.
                                        —Proverbs 4:6–7

O LORD, since you are my rock and my fortress,
  for the sake of your name lead and guide me.
                                        —Psalm 31:3

Lead me, O LORD, in your righteousness
  because of my enemies—
  make straight your way before me.

                                        —Psalm 5:8

The LORD loves the just
  and will not forsake his faithful ones.
                                        —Psalm 37:28

Test me, O LORD, and try me,
  examine my heart and my mind;
for your love is ever before me,
  and I walk continually in your truth.

—Psalm 26:2–3

Blessed are those who dwell in your house;
  they are ever praising you.
Blessed are those whose strength is in you,
  who have set their hearts on pilgrimage.

—Psalm 84:4–5

Here is my servant, whom I uphold,
  my chosen one in whom I delight;
I will put my Spirit on him
  and he will bring justice to the nations.

—Isaiah 42:1

The LORD said to me: "What they say is good. I will
raise up for them a prophet like you from among
their brothers; I will put my words in his mouth,
and he will tell them everything I command him.
If anyone does not listen to my words that the
prophet speaks in my name, I myself will call him
to account."

—Deuteronomy 18:17–19

Blessed are they who maintain justice,
who constantly do what is right.

—Psalm 106:3

Each of us will give an account of himself to God.

—Romans 14:12

Obey your leaders and submit to their authority.
They keep watch over you as men who must give
an account. Obey them so that their work will be
a joy, not a burden, for that would be of no
advantage to you. *—Hebrews 13:17*

The heart of the discerning acquires knowledge.

—Proverbs 18:15

Apply your heart to instruction
and your ears to words of knowledge.

—Proverbs 23:12

This is good, and pleases God our Savior, who
wants all men to be saved and to come to a
knowledge of the truth. *—1 Timothy 2:3–4*

A man of knowledge uses words with restraint,
and a man of understanding is even-tempered.

—Proverbs 17:27

Scriptures about Service

To me, to live is Christ and to die is gain. If I am to go on living in the body, this will mean fruitful labor for me. Yet what shall I choose? I do not know! I am torn between the two: I desire to depart and be with Christ, which is better by far; but it is more necessary for you that I remain in the body. Convinced of this, I know that I will remain, and I will continue with all of you for your progress and joy in the faith, so that through my being with you again your joy in Christ Jesus will overflow on account of me.   *—Philippians 1:21–26*

Serve wholeheartedly, as if you were serving the Lord, not men, because you know that the Lord will reward everyone for whatever good he does, whether he is slave or free.   *—Ephesians 6:7–8*

Whatever you do, work at it with all your heart, as working for the Lord, not for men, since you know that you will receive an inheritance from the Lord as a reward. It is the Lord Christ you are serving.
   —Colossians 3:23–24

Moses took his seat to serve as judge for the people, and they stood around him from morning till evening.   *—Exodus 18:13*

Be careful that you do not forget the LORD.... Fear the LORD your God, serve him only and take your oaths in his name.   —*Deuteronomy 6:12–13*

Moses' father-in-law replied, "What you are doing is not good. You and these people who come to you will only wear yourselves out. The work is too heavy for you; you cannot handle it alone. Listen now to me and I will give you some advice, and may God be with you. You must be the people's representative before God and bring their disputes to him. Teach them the decrees and laws, and show them the way to live and the duties they are to perform. But select capable men from all the people—men who fear God, trustworthy men who hate dishonest gain—and appoint them as officials over thousands, hundreds, fifties and tens. Have them serve as judges for the people at all times, but have them bring every difficult case to you; the simple cases they can decide themselves. That will make your load lighter, because they will share it with you. If you do this and God so commands, you will be able to stand the strain, and all these people will go home satisfied."

Moses listened to his father-in-law and did everything he said.   —*Exodus 18:17–24*

Scriptures about
SERVICE

The men [were] counted by Moses and Aaron and the twelve leaders of Israel, each one representing his family. All the Israelites twenty years old or more who were able to serve in Israel's army were counted according to their families.

–Numbers 1:44–45

God is able to make all grace abound to you, so that in all things at all times, having all that you need, you will abound in every good work.

–2 Corinthians 9:8

Welcome him in the Lord with great joy, and honor men like him, because he almost died for the work of Christ, risking his life.   –Philippians 2:29–30

Carry each others burdens, and in this way you will fufill the law of Christ.   –Galatians 6:2

Scriptures about Courage

Have I not commanded you? Be strong and courageous. Do not be terrified; do not be discouraged, for the LORD your God will be with you wherever you go. *—Joshua 1:9*

So keep up your courage, men, for I have faith in God that it will happen just as he told me.

—Acts 27:25

I can do everything through Christ who gives me strength. *—Philippians 4:13*

You may say to yourselves, "These nations are stronger than we are. How can we drive them out?" But do not be afraid of them; remember well what the LORD your God did to Pharaoh and to all Egypt. You saw with your own eyes the great trials, the miraculous signs and wonders, the mighty hand and outstretched arm, with which the LORD your God brought you out. The LORD your God will do the same to all the peoples you now fear.

—Deuteronomy 7:17–19

Act with courage, and may the LORD be with those who do well. *—2 Chronicles 19:11*

Scriptures about
COURAGE

Because the hand of the LORD my God was on me, I took courage. —*Ezra 7:28*

Be on your guard; stand firm in the faith; be men of courage; be strong. —*1 Corinthians 16:13*

I lift up my eyes to the hills—
    where does my help come from?
My help comes from the LORD,
    the Maker of heaven and earth.
He will not let your foot slip—
    he who watches over you will not slumber; . . .
The LORD watches over you—
    the LORD is your shade at your right hand;
the sun will not harm you by day,
    nor the moon by night.
The LORD will keep you from all harm—
    he will watch over your life;
the LORD will watch over your coming and going
    both now and forevermore.
                                    —*Psalm 121:1–3, 5–8*

The eyes of the LORD range throughout the earth to strengthen those whose hearts are fully committed to him. —*2 Chronicles 16:9*

God is our refuge and strength,
    an ever-present help in trouble.

—Psalm 46:1

The LORD surrounds his people
both now and forevermore.

—Psalm 125:2

God has said,
    "Never will I leave you;
    never will I forsake you."
So we say with confidence,
    "The Lord is my helper; I will not be afraid.
    What can man do to me?"

—Hebrews 13:5–6

He guards the course of the just
    and protects the way of his faithful ones.

—Proverbs 2:8

He is my loving God and my fortress,
    my stronghold and my deliverer,
    my shield, in whom I take refuge.

—Psalm 144:2

What, then, shall we say in response to this? If God
is for us, who can be against us? *—Romans 8:31*

Scriptures about
COURAGE

As for God, his way is perfect;
 the word of the LORD is flawless.
He is a shield
 for all who take refuge in him.
For who is God besides the LORD?
 And who is the Rock except our God?
It is God who arms me with strength
 and makes my way perfect.

—2 Samuel 22:31–33

The LORD your God is with you,
 he is mighty to save.
He will take great delight in you,
 he will quiet you with his love,
 he will rejoice over you with singing.

—Zephaniah 3:17

See, the LORD your God has given you the land. Go up and take possession of it as the LORD, the God of your fathers, told you. Do not be afraid; do not be discouraged.   *—Deuteronomy 1:21*

I will say of the LORD, "He is my refuge and
    my fortress,
  my God, in whom I trust."

—Psalm 91:2

Do not fear, for I am with you;
    do not be dismayed, for I am your God.
I will strengthen you and help you;
    I will uphold you with my righteous right hand.

—Isaiah 41:10

Be strong and courageous. Do not be afraid or
terrified because of them, for the LORD your God
goes with you; he will never leave you nor forsake
you.   *—Deuteronomy 31:6*

Reflections about Service

We do honor to the stars and stripes as the emblem of our country and the symbol of all that our patriotism means.

We identify the flag with almost everything we hold dear on earth. It represents our peace and security, our civil and political liberty, our freedom of religious worship, our family, our friends, our home. We see it in the great multitude of blessings, of rights and privileges that make up our country.

But when we look at our flag and behold it emblazoned with all our rights, we must remember that it is equally a symbol of our duties. Every glory that we associate with it is the result of duty done. A yearly contemplation of our flag strengthens and purifies the national conscience.

—*Calvin Coolidge*

It will be the purpose of my Administration to require the honest and faithful service of all executive officers, remembering that the offices were created, not for the benefit of incumbents or their supporters, but for the service of the Government. —*James A. Garfield*

If one asks me the meaning of our flag, I say to him: It means all that the Constitution of our people, organizing for justice, for liberty and for happiness, meant.

Our Flag carries American ideas, American history and American feelings.

This American Flag was the safeguard of liberty. It was an ordinance of liberty by the people, for the people. That it meant, that it means, and, by the blessing of God, that it shall mean to the end of time!
                                   —*Henry Ward Beecher*

So nigh is grandeur to our dust,
    So near is God to man,
When Duty whispers low, "Thou must,"
    The youth replies, "I can."

                                   —*Ralph Waldo Emerson*

Cast all your cares on God; that anchor holds.
                                   —*Alfred Lord Tennyson*

I enter on the trust to which I have been called by the suffrages of my fellow-citizens with my fervent prayers to the Almighty that He will be graciously pleased to continue to us that protection which He has already so conspicuously displayed in our favor.
                                   —*James Monroe*

With a firm reliance on the protection of Almighty
God, I shall forthwith commence the duties of the
high trust to which you have called me.

—James Monroe

I only look to the gracious protection of the Divine
Being whose strengthening support I humbly
solicit, and whom I fervently pray to look down
upon us all.

—Martin Van Buren

One flag, one land,
one heart, one hand,
One nation, evermore!

—Oliver Wendell Holmes

God loves America. When you consider what He
went through to bring our forebearers to this
magnificent land, and when you realize what He
accomplished in bringing forth a new nation on
this continent—a government founded on Christian
principles and dedicated to life, liberty, and the
pursuit of happiness—you have to realize that He
had a dramatic vision and purpose for this nation.

—James Kennedy

I therefore believe it is my duty to my Country to love it; to support its Constitution; to obey its laws; to respect its flag, and to defend it against all enemies.
                                        —*William Tyler Page*

And by the blessing of God may that country itself become a vast and splendid monument, not of oppression and terror, but of wisdom, of peace, and of liberty, upon which the world may gaze with admiration, forever.
                                        —*Daniel Webster*

No one should fear to undertake any task in the name of our Savior, if it is just and if the intention is purely for His holy service. The working out of all things has been assigned to each person by our Lord, but it all happens according to His sovereign will even though He gives advice.
                                        —*Christopher Columbus*

Because of what America is and what America has done, a firmer courage, a higher hope, inspires the heart of all humanity.
                                        —*Calvin Coolidge*

Above all, we must realize that no arsenal, or no weapon in the arsenals of the world, is so formidable as the will and moral courage of free men and women.
                                        —*Ronald Reagan*

America, the Beautiful

O beautiful for spacious skies,
For amber waves of grain,
For purple mountain majesties
Above the fruited plain!
America! America! God shed His grace on thee,
And crown thy good with brotherhood
From sea to shining sea.

O beautiful for heroes proved
In liberating strife,
Who more than self their country loved
And mercy more than life!
America! America! May God thy gold refine,
Till all success be nobleness,
And ev'ry gain divine.

O beautiful for patriot dream
That sees, beyond the years,
Thine alabaster cities gleam—
Undimmed by human tears!
America! America! God shed His grace on thee,
And crown thy good with brotherhood
From sea to shining sea.

—Katherine Lee Bates

Reflections about
SERVICE

No country is more loved by its people. I have an abiding faith in their capacity, integrity and high purpose. *–Herbert Hoover*

It is the duty of nations, as well as of men, to own their dependence upon the overruling power of God and to recognize the sublime truth announced in the Holy Scriptures and proven by all history, that those nations only are blessed whose God is the Lord. *–Abraham Lincoln*

I appear, my fellow-citizens, in your presence and in that of Heaven to bind myself by the solemnities of religious obligation to the faithful performance of the duties allotted to me in the station to which I have been called. *–John Quincy Adams*

I shall have no motive to influence my conduct in administering the Government except the desire ably and faithfully to serve my country and to live in grateful memory of my countrymen.

–James Buchanan

The great essential to our happiness and prosperity is that we adhere to the principles upon which the Government was established and insist upon their faithful observance. *–William McKinley*

Reflections about
SERVICE

Faith of Our Fathers

Faith of our fathers! Living still
In spite of dungeon, fire, and sword:
Oh how our hearts beat high with joy
When-e'er we hear that glorious word!
Faith of our fathers! holy faith!
We will be true to thee till death!

—Frederick W. Faber

My great passion for America is twofold: first, that
every believer would be absolutely faithful to the
Great Commission; and then, that every believer
would take seriously the challenge to reclaim this
nation for Christ. If we become engaged and if we
carry out the "cultural mandate" of the church,
then there is no reason that we cannot reclaim our
heritage of faith and freedom and see this nation
renewed. *—James Kennedy*

A Christian man is the most free lord of all, and
subject to none; a Christian man is the most dutiful
servant of all, and subject to everyone.

—Martin Luther

The noblest service comes from nameless hands.
And the best servant does his work unseen.

—Oliver Wendell Holmes

I shall look for whatever success may attend my public service; and knowing that "except the Lord keep the city the watchman waketh but in vain," with fervent supplications for His favor, to His overruling providence I commit with humble but fearless confidence my own fate and the future destinies of my country.   —*John Quincy Adams*

I ask the help of Almighty God in this service to my country to which you have called me.
   —*Herbert Hoover*

Service is the supreme commitment of life.
   —*Warren G. Harding*

The obligation I am under to my countrymen for the great honor they have conferred on me by returning me to the highest office within their gift, and the further obligation resting on me to render to them the best services within my power.
   —*Ulysses S. Grant*

As Americans, we go forward, in the service of our country, by the will of God.   —*Franklin D. Roosevelt*

Be alert to give service. What counts a great deal in life is what we do for others.   —*Anonymous*

Reflections about
SERVICE

"The Star-Spangled Banner"

During the War of 1812, the British captured the city of Washington, setting fire to the Capitol building and the White House.

In the blaze of cannon fire, Francis Scott Key, a lawyer living in Georgetown, could still see an American flag waving over Fort McHenry. When the bombing suddenly stopped during that night, he had no way of knowing if the flag was still there or if the American stronghold had fallen to the British. But at dawn the American flag became visible, still intact over the fort.

Key was inspired to write a poem. His brother-in-law took it to a printer and copies were circulated around the city.

"The Star-Spangled Banner" was adopted as our national anthem on March 3, 1931.

The Star-Spangled Banner

Oh, say can you see, by the dawn's early light,
What so proudly we hailed at the twilight's last
    gleaming,
Whose broad stripes and bright stars through the
    perilous fight,
O'er the ramparts we watched were so gallantly
    streaming?
And the rockets' red glare, the bombs bursting in
    air,
Gave proof thro' the night that our flag was still
    there.
Oh, say, does that star-spangled banner yet wave
O'er the land of the free, and the home of the
    brave!

Oh, thus be it ever when freeman shall stand
Between their loved homes and the war's
    desolation;
Blest with victory and peace, may the heaven-
    rescued land
Praise the power that hath made and preserved us
    a nation!
Then conquer we must, when our cause it is just,
And this be our motto: "In God is our trust!"
And the star-spangled banner in triumph doth
    wave,
O'er the land of the free, and the home of the
    brave!
                              —*Francis Scott Key*

U.S. FLAG–FOLDING CEREMONY

The flag–folding ceremony described by the *Uniformed Services Code* is a dramatic and uplifting way to honor the United States flag on special days, like Memorial Day or Veterans Day, and is sometimes used at retirement ceremonies and funerals.

The following is to be read as Honor Guard or Flag Detail is coming forward:

"The flag–folding ceremony represents the same religious principles on which our country was originally founded. The portion of the flag denoting honor is the canton of blue containing the stars representing the states our veterans served in uniform. The canton field of blue dresses from left to right and is inverted when draped as a pall on a casket of a veteran who has served our country in uniform.

"In the Armed Forces of the United States, at the ceremony of retreat the flag is lowered, folded in a triangle fold and kept under watch throughout the night as a tribute to our nation's honored dead. The next morning it is brought out and, at the ceremony of reveille, run aloft as a symbol of our belief in the resurrection of the body."

U. S. Flag-Folding Ceremony

Wait for the Honor Guard or Flag Detail to unravel and fold the flag into a quarter fold—resume reading when Honor Guard is standing ready:

"**The first fold** of our flag is a symbol of life.

"**The second fold** is a symbol of our belief in the eternal life.

"**The third fold** is made in honor and remembrance of the veteran departing our ranks who gave a portion of life for the defense of our country to attain a peace throughout the world.

"**The fourth fold** represents our weaker nature, for as American citizens trusting in God, it is to Him we turn in times of peace as well as in times of war for His divine guidance.

"**The fifth fold** is a tribute to our country, for in the words of Stephen Decatur, 'Our country, in dealing with other countries, may she always be right; but it is still our country, right or wrong.'

"**The sixth fold** is for where our hearts lie. It is with our heart that we pledge allegiance to the flag of the United States of America, and to the republic

U. S. Flag-Folding Ceremony

for which it stands, one nation, under God, indivisible, with liberty and justice for all.

"**The seventh fold** is a tribute to our Armed Forces, for it is through the Armed Forces that we protect our country and our flag against all her enemies, whether they be found within or without the boundaries of our republic.

"**The eighth fold** is a tribute to the one who entered into the valley of the shadow of death, that we might see the light of day, and to honor mother, for whom it flies on Mother's Day.

"**The ninth fold** is a tribute to womanhood; for it has been through their faith, love, loyalty and devotion that the character of the men and women who have made this country great have been molded.

"**The tenth fold** is a tribute to father, for he, too, has given his sons and daughters for the defense of our country since they were first born.

"**The eleventh fold**, in the eyes of a Hebrew citizen, represents the lower portion of the seal of King David and King Solomon, and glorifies, in their eyes, the God of Abraham, Isaac, and Jacob.

U. S. FLAG-FOLDING CEREMONY

"**The twelfth fold**, in the eyes of a Christian citizen, represents an emblem of eternity and glorifies, in their eyes, God the Father, the Son, and Holy Ghost.

When the flag is completely folded, the stars are uppermost, reminding us of our national motto, 'In God We Trust.'"

Wait for the Honor Guard or Flag Detail to inspect the flag—after the inspection, resume reading:

"After the flag is completely folded and tucked in, it takes on the appearance of a cocked hat, ever reminding us of the soldiers who served under General George Washington and the sailors and marines who served under Captain John Paul Jones who were followed by their comrades and shipmates in the Armed Forces of the United States, preserving for us the rights, privileges, and freedoms we enjoy today."

Sources

America's God and Country. William J. Federer. Coppell, TX: Fame Publishing, 1994

Benjamin Franklin's The Art of Virtue. Benjamin Franklin. George L. Rogers, editor. Acorn Publishing 1996

The Carpenter's Apprentice: The Spiritual Biography of Jimmy Carter. Dan Ariail and Cheryl Heckler-Feltz. Grand Rapids, MI: Zondervan Publishing House, 1996

Chaplain Service Institute *Book of Prayers*

Character & Destiny. D. James Kennedy with Jim Nelson Black. Grand Rapids, MI: Zondervan Publishing House, 1994

The Christian's Secret of a Holy Life. Hannah Whitall Smith, edited by Melvin E. Dieter. Grand Rapids, MI: Zondervan Publishing House, 1994

The Complete Speakers Sourcebook. Eleanor Doan. Grand Rapids, MI: Zondervan Publishing House, 1996

The Concordia Hymnal. Minneapolis, MN: Augsburg Publishing House, 1932

Charles Colson, Prison Fellowship Ministries. 1998

Daily Readings From Luther's Writings. Martin Luther, selected and edited by Barbara Owen. Minneapolis, MN: Augsburg Fortress, 1993

Edward Dobson. Calvary Church, 1998

The Encyclopedia of Religious Quotations. Edited and compiled by Frank S. Mead. Westwood, NJ: Fleming H. Revell Co., 1966

The Family Album of Favorite Poems. Edited by P. Edward Ernest. New York: Grosset & Dunlap Publishers, 1959

God's Little Instruction Book. Tulsa, OK: Honor Books, 1994

The Gospel of Life. Pope John Paul II, Encyclical Letter, Rome, March 25, 1995. New York: Random House, 1995

The Granger Anthology Series I The World's Best Poetry volume X. Great Neck, NY: Granger Book Co., Inc., 1982

The International Thesaurus of Quotations. Rhoda Thomas Tripp. Thomas Y. Crowell, 1970

The Joy of Words. Chicago, IL: J. G. Ferguson Publishing Co., 1960

Just As I Am. Billy Graham. Billy Graham Evangelistic Association. New York: Harper Collins/Zondervan, 1997

Keys to a Deeper Life. A. W. Tozer. Grand Rapids, MI: Creation House, Zondervan Publishing House, 1984

The Living Insights Study Bible, New International Version. Charles R. Swindoll, General Editor. Grand Rapids, MI: Zondervan Publishing House, 1996

Michigan Prayer Guide

Moving Through Your Problems Toward Finding God. Larry Crabb. Grand Rapids, MI: Zondervan, 1993

Operation World. Patrick J StG Johnstone. Grand Rapids, MI: Zondervan Publishing House, 1993

The Power of a Dream. Wintley Phipps with Goldie Down. Grand Rapids, MI: Zondervan Publishing House, 1994

Prayer. Charles R. Swindoll. Grand Rapids, MI: Zondervan Publishing House, 1995

The Prayers of Peter Marshall. Peter Marshall. New York: McGraw-Hill Chosen Books, 1954

Praise! Our Songs and Hymns. Compiled by John W. Peterson and Norman Johnson, and edited by Norman Johnson. Singspiration Music, 1979

Prayer Powerpoints. Compiled by Randall D. Roth. Wheaton, IL: Victor Books/SP Publications, 1995

Quiet Strength. Rosa Parks with Gregory Reed. Grand Rapids, MI: Zondervan Publishing House, 1994

The Quotable New Woman. Compiled by Elaine Partnow. New York: Pinnacle, 1977

Respectfully Quoted Library of Congress. Edited by Suzy Platte. Congressional Quarterly Publication, 1992

Revival Fire. Wesley Duewel. Grand Rapids, MI: Zondervan Publishing House, 1995

Roaring Lambs. Bob Briner. Grand Rapids, MI: Zondervan Publishing House, 1993

The Shorter Bartlett's Familiar Quotations. John Bartlett. New York: Pocket Books, Inc., 1965

Springs in the Valley. Mrs. Charles E. Cowman. Grand Rapids, MI: Zondervan Publishing House, 1968

Standing Firm. Dan Quayle. New York: HarperCollins/Zondervan, 1994

Under Fire: An American Story. Oliver North. New York: HarperCollins/Zondervan, 1991